[SERVING]

AS A BIVOCATIONAL PASTOR

POSITIVE HELP FOR A
GROWING MINISTRY

DR. JAMES W. HIGHLAND

NEWBURGH PRESS

Newburgh Press

ISBN: 978-0-9790625-5-1

Printed in the United States of America

This is in invitation to a conversation with a veteran pastor and church consultant, Dr. Jim Highland, about the challenges of serving as a bivocational pastor. The dreams, the delights and the difficulties are discussed. Join me…!

THE BIVOCATIONAL PASTOR

A Conversation With A Veteran

Dr. James W. Highland

Hello! Can we talk?

This book is written to be helpful to ministers who are serving as a bivocational pastor or are considering that ministry role. This is not an exhausting study of the role, but an imagined conversation with you about the key functions and challenges of the bivocational pastor.

In my experiences of being a pastor, consultant, personal counselor and friend of pastors, I understand the delights and difficulties of ministry. In my current roles of bivocational pastor and fundraising among churches for a statewide ministry, I understand the challenges that bivocational pastors face and want to share with you a down to earth conversation from my experience and perspective. With each chapter is a list of resource books, helpful materials and a related sermon.

Join me in a conversation about the bivocational pastor, a way to enhance your ministry and our Savior, Jesus Christ.

Thank you for joining me!

THE AUTHOR

Dr. James W. (Jim) Highland is a veteran in ministry. His career includes pastor of significant churches, Capital Funds Consultant to more than 200 churches, Executive Vice-President of a nationally recognized church fundraising company, presently Bivocational Pastor of a small rural church and Development Director of a Tennessee Baptist Convention agency.

CONTENTS

Chapter 1: Ministry in Today's World.................3

"you have come into the kingdom for such a time as this." Esther 4:14

Chapter 2: When God Calls...................................19

"Make your salvation and calling sure." II Peter 2:10

Chapter 3: Serving Christ Through His Church

....47

"I will build my church and the gates of hell shall not overcome it." Matthew 16:18

Chapter 4: The Bivocational Preacher.............69

"It pleased God by the foolishness of preaching to save those who believe." I Corinthians 1:21

Chapter 5: The Bivocational Pastor...................91

"It was He who gave some to be. . .pastor. . .to prepare God's people for the works of the service so that the church may be built up." Ephesians 4:11

Chapter 6: The Bivocational Leader................121

"A Leader is not a person who can to do the work better than others. He is a person who can get others to do the work better than he can."

CHAPTER 7: THE BIVOCATIONAL PASTOR WORKING WITH OTHERS...143

"12 And we urge you, brethren, to recognize those who labor among you, and are over you in the Lord and admonish you, 13 and to esteem them very highly in love for their work's sake. Be at peace among yourselves." 1 Thessalonians 5:12-13

CHAPTER 8: THE BIVOCATIONAL PASTOR, FINANCES AND COMPENSATION..163

"I know how to be abased, and I know how to abound. Everywhere and in all things I have learned both to be full and to be hungry, both to abound and to suffer need." Philippians 4:12

CHAPTER 9: THE BIVOCATIONAL PASTOR, PERSONAL LIFE ISSUES..183

"11 Only Luke is with me. Get Mark and bring him with you, for he is useful to me for ministry. 12 And Tychicus I have sent to Ephesus. 13 Bring the cloak that I left with Carpus at Troas when you come—and the books, especially the parchments." II Timothy 4:11-13

CHAPTER 10: THE BIVOCATIONAL PASTOR AND A BALANCED LIFE..209

"I have fought a good fight, I have finished my course, I have kept the faith." 2 Timothy 4:6-8

RESOURCES
SERMONS:

There are sermons or other resource following the chapters that relate to the theme of that chapter. Read them as a personal message to the reader. Feel free to use any of the material in your own ministry. Most of our sermons and programs unintentionally include materials from other preacher's materials, and these may be also.

[VISION]

MINISTER IN TODAY'S WORLD, EMBRACING CHANGE AND TRADITION

CHAPTER ONE:

BIVOCATIONAL MINISTRY IN TODAY'S WORLD

"You have come into the kingdom
for such a time as this."

ESTHER 4:14

A familiar sentence in the conversation of two men (sometimes women) when they meet and begin learning to know each other is, "What do you do?" Translated they mean, "What is your work, job or vocation?" Guys usually start there. Ministry oriented guys usually think of one of several traditional areas: preacher, music minister, education minister, etc.

My answer is, "I am a Bivocational Pastor and a Development Director for a Tennessee Baptist Convention organization." Then we move on to the details. I am pastor of New Bethel Baptist Church located seven miles out from Shelbyville, Tennessee. At the time of this writing I have served there for five years.

"Bivocational pastor…" What's that? Years ago, we were called "part-time preachers" or "weekend warriors." Most of the time, these were persons who responded to God's call to ministry later in adulthood, often had little opportunity to gain further education in Bible and theology, and maintained a second job to survive financially. They had usually served in volunteer leadership roles in a church and served with the natural abilities, social skills and Biblical understanding they had gathered in their earlier life. They seldom had the opportunity to further their education full-time, considering the circumstances of their family, their finances and their present vocational options. They were seen as persons who could not qualify for being "full-time, full salary" positions but always sincere. Their usual path was to find a small church needing a pastor, seek the support and guidance of fellow pastors and denominational leaders and begin their ministry. Soon the biggest challenge was sermons to be prepared every week, leadership roles to perform and people issues to negotiate.

The reality is that the dynamics of our nation and world are reshaping our world's churches and personal lives. We can wrap most of these dynamics into one word, "change", and the larger phrase "speed of change." "Change" is impacting every area of our lives, but there are some key areas where we confront it constantly. Take communication, for instance! The speed of knowing the news has gone from overnight to same-day, then within the hour to seconds. That's news from anywhere on the globe!

We are all experiencing the "speed of change." No one wants to wait any more, including myself. We buy an automobile in an hour, a house in one day, a letter is exchanged in five minutes and read the latest news only five to ten minutes after it happens. This creates a hurried life and we don't know what to do when we have leisure time. Some other factors in my "hurry up and wait" lifestyle is that our conversations with persons and organizations around the world is always on-going. We are always in contact with a global community. The diversity of racial and religious backgrounds and thoughts is accepted as normal. Fasten your seatbelt; it's only going to be faster.

Again, think about the speed of changes in church ministry. The pace of life is almost frantic for some of us, busy for all of us. It's hard to do family ministry to our members when they are never at home. Church members are acting out their commitment decisions by giving a handful of hours each week, one to two hours each Sunday or making an occasional visit to church on weekdays. We can interpret their financial support in the same ways. So the stewardship of time and money are key discipleship issues. It's enough to make one give up and go home! But this is both our ministry field and our mission field and the fields are "white unto harvest." We cannot go back to yesterday's way of being and doing church because that's like living in the grave yard. God's direction for us is always "forward." We cannot avoid that our calling and ministry is not to yesterday but to tomorrow. Scott Peck, in his book "The Road Less Traveled" advises that "avoidance is always the beginning of mental illness." You and I both know persons and groups of persons called church who are ill in that way.

As a minister/pastor, this is the world you will be working in throughout your ministry. "You have come into God's Kingdom for such a time as this." Many other changes that you may have already made peace with are impacting our lives. A simple one is to realize we now are ministering to four distinct generations where each generation thinks and talks differently, want different things done and can't understand why the other generations can't see things their way. Social and economic changes are gradually creating a widening gulf between the rich and the poor. Churches and attitudes about churches are changing with a blending of many beliefs, cultures and practices into a beige-colored institution. The most obvious result of all of those factors is our declining ability to communicate with each other. These changes cause most of us to draw into our safe place and become polarized when trying to communicate. Someone told me that many of us create our ideas like harden clay marbles, carry them around in our pockets of head and heart, pull them out to show to others who we think would appreciate them and put them safely back into our pockets.

The speed of changes makes personal time more valuable, which changes how we do relationships and church. Gradually churches are discarding the mid-week services, then the Sunday evening services and meet for worship and fellowship only once each week. In addition to that, the average person or family make a decision on whether they will invest one or two hours on Sunday morning. Some of the best times of Christian fellowship, unstructured times and informal gatherings, are not practiced in most churches.

Time is what life is made of, and we choose how we will invest it. The bivocational pastor will certainly encounter the pressure of giving time to family, friendships, small groups, study, prayer and personal leisure time. As a bivocational pastor, you will be expected to adjust to many of these challenges. That may require both changes in attitudes and preaching.

Another challenging factor in serving as a bivocational pastor is that we serve people who are very mobile. Depending on where you are serving, people may be very transitional (around a military base or college campus), or not very transitional (as in an older, established community.") This impacts available leaders, dependable attendance and the giving patterns of people.

An area of change that impacts most of the persons in the church is the use of new technology today. This will include the use of computers, cell phones, visual equipment in the worship place and the ability of the groups to accept and use them. As an older person, I am constantly learning how to use new computer tools.

But you and I have been called to serve at such a time as this. We cannot dial back to another time or age, and we cannot expect people we work with to either catch up or dumb-down to accommodate us. When Jesus spoke about going into all the world, He was not just talking geography, but worlds of different customs, languages, religious backgrounds and morality. We can take confidence that it has been done before, in every age of our world, and God has blessed those in the past to be effective for Him. He will do the same for us!

Let's look at the bigger issues of church functioning in our cultures. There are at least four levels of churches that are operating today: The mega churches, the large churches, the medium churches and the smaller churches. Although it would be hard to specifically place all churches in one of these groups, we can cluster the various kinds of smaller churches in one level. In this book we will primarily talk about smaller churches where bivocational pastors are serving. In the chapter, "Understanding the Church in These Times," we will reflect the characteristics and challenges of serving these churches.

The largest challenge in the smaller church groups is the negative power of the economy. The financial resources of these churches are growing smaller even as the cost of operating the church is growing larger. While there are financial cuts that can be made for churches diminishing in size, the churches that are stable or growing are financially challenged.

The most obvious financial cutback area is in staff persons, moving most ministry staff roles from full-time/full-support to part-time/bivocational. This stretches the pool of capable, committed bivocational ministers very slim. In this group are active, prepared bivocational pastors and retired pastors. The need for trained, capable and committed bivocational pastors is huge.

A big area of consideration will be the role of the bivocational pastor in these churches. My assumptions are that if you have picked up this book, you are either a bivocational pastor or are considering becoming one. You have many questions on what you should do, how you do it and is that what God wants you to do. We will dig into the dynamics of church life and the bivocational pastor's role of pastor and leader. These areas of exploration will lead us to think about how to work with others and how to give pastoral care. We will naturally follow these with the personal issues of bivocational ministers, managing time, money, family, personal health, spiritual and career growth, and how we present ourselves to others. Last, we will consider how to face these challenges. Let's get going!

RECOMMENDED RESOURCES
FOR THIS CHAPTER

Anderson, Leith (1998). *Dying For Change:* Bethany House Publishers.

Dale, Robert D. (2004). *Keeping the Dream Alive:* Broadman Press.

Schaller, Lyle E. (1996). *The New Reformation:* Abingdon Press.

Sweet, Leonard (1995). *Faithquakes:* Abingdon Press.

Woods, C. Jeff (1996). *Congregational Megatrends:* The Alban Institute

SERMON RESOURCE

Beyond the Boundary of Impossible

JOHN 6:1 -13

Our lives are filled and often controlled by boundaries. A property owner can point out his property line and call those who cross it "trespassers." The highway patrolman cruises the public roads and looks for those who exceed the speed limit and writes a ticket charging "speeding." We each have boundaries for our physical abilities and social interaction. Our families are in the practice of labeling some things "possible" and other things "impossible." Those are mental file labels for us, choosing those things that are realistically, rationally and achievably "possible." We mentally file many things that don't fit that criteria "impossible."

This event of feeding 5,000 was more for the benefit of the disciples than the hungry crowd. The disciples had returned from their first mission trip without Jesus and described the events by saying, "I saw Satan fall." They had watched Jesus do many mighty things, healing and changing minds. Now they must settle down into a very hard period of their lives. Jesus was beginning to face boldly the reality of a criminal death, while his disciples knew of his ideas and said "impossible." So much was not only possible but it was also very close to happening.

Both the disciples and Jesus needed a few hours or days for a "rest retreat." Jesus loaded them into a boat and left for a quiet place across the lake on a secluded hillside. Just as they settled in at a place to talk, a huge crowd estimated to be 8,000-10,000 people appeared. They had walked around the lake, seeking to hear Jesus and see people healed.

After a brief time of teaching, Jesus involved his disciples in making a big decision. Should they dismiss the crowd to go home or make plans to feed them? Phillip, the realist, reported that it would take the equivalent of six month's salary for labor, or $20,000, to feed them. Andrew, the optimist, suggested the only food he had discovered among the crowd was a small peasant boy's lunch bag, five small barley loaves or biscuits and two small fish. His evaluating comment about the lunch was, "But what are they among so many?"

This is one of seven miracles, or signs that John chose to build his descriptions of the ministry of Jesus. Different from the other three gospels, John wrote his more than forty years after the death and resurrection of Jesus. While the others wrote a chronological account of Jesus' life, John wrote about the essence of the life of Jesus. He stated his purpose was to lead people "to believe that Jesus was the Christ and that believing they might have life in His name." (John 20:2). To do this he chose seven unique miracles that he called "signs." Like a road sign, they said something, gave a message and declared the truth about Jesus. Although there are several themes that are common to all the miracles, a very dominate one was the way Jesus turned the impossible into a possible reality. This is the only miracle that is included in all four gospels, but John lifts it from being a feeding of the five thousand to the necessary training of the twelve disciples. Let's look at the process Jesus used to both feed the multitude and train the disciples.

Jesus chose to start with what he had.

We might want to wait until we receive more resources to begin such a big project. Many of us talk about doing things "if only." If only we have the money, time opportunity or help. Jesus began with the boy's lunch. As Andrew had said, "What is this among so many people?" It had to be faith, and a close companionship with the Spirit, to launch out without the needed resources.

Jesus asked them to be seated in orderly groups, in anticipation that the disciples would serve. He built the setting in which a miracle could happen. He prepared the disciples to participate in a miracle. While some skeptics have reasoned that everyone had enough food for themselves but were selfishly hiding it. Only when the boy chose to give his lunch did everyone else take out their food and produce enough food for everyone with some left over. This was not a miracle of sharing but a God-sent miracle of feeding 8,000 – 10,000 far away from any store or source of food. Jesus prepared them for a miracle.

Jesus first blessed the food.

"Jesus took the bread and gave thanks." He then began to serve it. He did the same with the fish. This sounds like what he did at the last supper where He was personally to be the gift being offered to mankind. Jesus was inviting God to come and feed them. He was inviting those eating to participate in a real miracle. We need to learn to pray in faith, when the reality of our prayers have not been answered yet. When we come to times of need, we can trust God to provide. The scripture teaches us to pray, for "all things are possible."

Jesus started serving the food.

Remember the disciples were serving the food, going to Jesus to receive the food and taking it to the groups. Can you imagine what they were watching? The food coming from the boy's lunch was always available and never ran out. The resources were always there when the disciples came back for more. It was an impossibility happening before their eyes. Remember the first miracle in John at the wedding? Jesus took ordinary water and made it into extraordinary wine and the wine never ran out. Impossibilities became realities at the hand of Jesus.

Finally. there is a teachable moment at the last.

Jesus commanded the disciples to gather up all the leftovers. "Let nothing be wasted," He said. Twelve baskets full were gathered. I've always wondered how big the baskets were, where did the baskets come from to start with? Maybe that was a "guess…" they had for how much could be gathered in a headdress wrapping or another piece of clothing. However, it was measured and there were twelve baskets full. That was enough to give each disciple one basketful to emphasize that "with God all things are possible."

Can you see them there, sitting and looking at the big baskets of leftovers and rethinking their initial conclusions?

This miracle, or sign, shouts a message! There are no boundary lines on what is possible and impossible with God. Perhaps the old saying is worth repeating, "Those who say something can't be done should get out of the way of those doing it," with God's help.

[CALLING]

ACCEPTING SURRENDER, LIFELONG LEARNING AND THE COURAGE TO SERVE

CHAPTER TWO:

WHEN GOD CALLS

"Make your salvation and calling sure"
II Peter 2:10

Being "called" sounds like some mysterious and inde-finable experience. Some see it as a special badge we can wear to enable us to have unusual powers and per-ception. (Like a member of an orchestra resting while everyone else is busy tuning up for the concert. When asked why he was not so busy, he said, "They are look-ing for it; I've found it.") Some use that special badge to place themselves in a superior position over others.

God's mode of operation has been to "call" people from the routine of life to give leadership in His work and plans. A brief Biblical overview of God's call in the lives of persons He has used is most interesting in its diversity. God called Abram to start a new nation but Abram took years to get in the position to do that. God called Paul to be His first missionary to the Gentiles like us and he immediately prepared to do this. God sent him on a three year retreat for him to reshape his theology so he could serve effectively.

God called Noah to build an ark to save the people and animals of the earth so He could start over with mankind so called a carpenter to execute His plan. God called a doctor named Luke to be the personal physician to Paul. We have no quoted words of Luke but we have two major books of the New Testament (Luke, Acts), written by Luke that quickly became part of the education resources for new Christians and churches.

God called prophets like Isaiah and Jeremiah to speak to the needs of their dying nation. He called John the Baptist to announce that the new Israel was launched with the coming of Jesus. I encourage you to visit each of the Bible passages describing God's call on people's lives and consider the patterns they have in common.

As I have reflected on my own experience of calling and listened to others, I observe three steps or phases that are usually apparent. Please keep in mind that God seldom does the same things alike and each person's experience is unique to them. I have intentionally chosen to describe my thoughts in non-Biblical or spiritual language. Often we get bogged down on the spiritual vocabulary that fits some of us, but not all of us.

The first of these steps I call "a sense of oughtness."

Who among us has not experienced "oughtness" when we go by a stranded person and feel we should do something to help them. Many times we have sensed God is leading us to make a step forward spiritually or volunteer to do something for others. I realize a sense of "oughtness" can also come from guilt or the need to be noticed, but I speak of a more genuine sense. Because each of us is made so different from others, the call of God upon our lives must be especially fitted to us.

Often that sense of oughtness is more a sense of possibility. Many of us feel that God could not really use us, and we fill in the blanks in our mind as to why this could never happen to us. Many of us who enter ministry consider ourselves average or less, not of great value or potential. One of the remarkable things about God's choice to use us is that He takes average persons to work and guide in extraordinary realms of His kingdom. Many of us in ministry are in awe that God could take a regular guy like ourselves and place us in key places to serve Him in His kingdom.

One of the response options we have is to refuse the invitation. Sometimes this happens simply by keeping the clutter of our lives very active and refusing to consider the invitation. We've all met people who "recall" an invitation coming into their lives earlier, but refused it by not giving it any serious consideration.

A second response option for us is to put the invitation "on hold," to decide to "wait and see." There is a sense that callings such as this, one that will definitely take control of our lives, needs to be approached carefully. All of us are different in how we make decisions. A minority of us are "early adopters," ready to embrace new ideas enthusiastically. On the other end of the scale, a minority of us are "late adopters," choosing to wait until others have decided and play things safe. The middle group, perhaps 60%, looks at leadership from others and makes their decisions gradually. I know more late adopters who fail to make the right decision and are sorry, than the early adapters who have made the wrong decisions. Ultimately, everyone who senses the call of God on their life is most blessed by being an early adopter.

Sometimes the sense of oughtness becomes mixed with many other options that we confidently see as possibilities in our lives. We may be in a fulfilling, successful career when the "oughtness sense" comes calling. The call of God upon our lives is not a "when all else fails" choice or the last best option. The Apostle Paul was not a person ready to fall through the cracks, but an aggressive, successful leader of Jewish politics.

However, when that sense of oughtness arrives in our life, we must deal with it. Often we are surprised by its presence and will need to get used to that open question in our lives. I'm sure we all agree that the source of that oughtness is the Holy Spirit, the Spirit of Jesus. This is God's invitation to join His forces, engage with Him in work and invest our lives in eternal matters. His presence will keep that "oughtness" active until we respond with a "yes" or try to smother the "oughtness" to death.

The third exciting response option is to open your life to God's invitation. In this option you will not have your questions answered. You have even more precise, but positive, questions.

"What specifically is God calling me to do, but whatever it is, I say yes." The "yes" in your life allows God to begin to show you the next steps in your process. The "yes" in your life discards all confusion from the past decision-making journey. It puts you on the road to discovering God's will and way of your life.

The second part of God's call is what I call "growing enthusiasm." Like our experience of salvation, a key test of sincerity in our "yes" response is our growing enthusiasm for the decision. The person who has accepted Jesus as their Savior and is reluctant to acknowledge Him, has a serious problem. The same is true of God's call. We must remove the bridles of reluctance and begin to think freely of what God is doing in our lives. A God-instigated call is more dominantly on our mind, and we experience growing enthusiasm for the possibilities in our life. When we share this with others and they respond positively, we begin to see ourselves doing this.

The third level of our calling experience is that of "confirming experiences." I'm not talking about "laying out the fleece." That practice requires receiving a "yes or no" answer. These can be as simple as the response of a trusted, credible acquaintance or a moment when an action affirms the decision. But remember, your invitation by God and your acceptance of His calling are facts, locked in our mind, affirmed by our emotions and confirmed by events or persons independent from the journey you have traveled. Please read this description as a generic exploration of God's call on our lives. Your experiences will be more specific, more personal and more spirit-led than these words.

When God Calls - To Prepare. God's calling may be for a specific mission or action, and you could take the same path to answer that call. This may be God's call to Jeremiah to take his specific message of judgment to the king, or God's call for John the Baptist to condemn the king because of his immoral life.

Most often God's call to us is to surrender our life to His work. Jesus called his disciples to "follow me" and He called the Apostle Paul to be a missionary to the gentiles. In every case I can find, His call is also a call to prepare. Jesus called His disciples to follow Him for three years before He turned His earthly ministry over to them. Jesus' call to Paul on the Damascus Road was a call to retreat to a wilderness and prepare for the world mission being launched. While Paul was the most educated in theology of all Christian advocates, the most gifted in speaking and the most experienced in moving through the Jewish religions, Paul needed to prepare. After Paul was converted, he tried to witness to fellow Christians and former Jewish peers. He failed miserably. It took Paul three long years in a wilderness setting to rethink his theology to be Christ-centered, adjust his culture to include gentiles and to change his world boundaries to include "the entire world."

You and I need time and space to adjust our minds and hearts to include the knowledge and application of the gospel in the ministry He has for us. All of us come to our calling with a mixture of traditional Bible knowledge, cultural, social understandings and personal gifts. The most important components we have in this mix are our experience of trusting Jesus as Savior and our calling to ministry.

Education is a life-long pursuit in ministry. Paul underscores this for Timothy when he advised him to *"study to show yourself approved unto God, a workman that needeth not to be ashamed"* (2 Timothy 2:15). Our calling urges us to prepare. This is one of a handful of key commitments we make. There is the immediate preparation of a sermon or Bible study, and also continued preparation to be a faithful leader, pastor and representative of Jesus. This is like playing golf; you play the ball where it lies. Some of us come to this moment with good academic preparation, while some of us come starting not only a life of ministry but a life of basic learning. All of us will have blanks, gaps and misinformation.

Our goal is not to be just average. The goal of ministry is to offer our best to God, to *"submit yourself as a sacrifice unto God, which is your reasonable service"* (Romans 12:1). Our calling often comes at inconvenient times in our lives. We need to maintain a job and support and care for a family while we find a way to prepare. Many will begin to explore the opportunities available. Southern Baptist Associations offer courses in Bible and ministry skills where you can earn seminary credits. Others will go on-line for institutions that offer on-line classes for credit toward a degree. One that I recommend enthusiastically is Newburg Bible College and Seminary in Evansville, Indiana. My wife and I have worked with Newbury Seminary to offer special seminar learning experiences to add to their excellent Bible, theology, and ministry skills development, all with the ability to earn degrees. They have enrolled more than 2,500 students in the past ten years with more than 250 students graduating each year. (www.newburgseminary.com)

An essential part of preparation is participating in peer group support and working with a mentor. A group of fellow bivocational pastors can be found in most communities that will welcome a new member. There are many pastors, retired or in service, who will gladly invest in your ministry as a mentor. Your local denominational worker or leading pastor will help you connect to these resourceful persons.

There are skills and attitudes to be developed that will serve you best in ministry. Some of the essential skills may already be developed in your life: speaking, studying, social, and care-giving skills. If not, there are resources and resourceful people available if you seek them out. Attitudes are very important to the effectiveness of your ministry. While it is essential that we have firmly held convictions about some things, we must also have flexible spirits and loving acceptance of the many people we minister to.

Called - To A Specific Church. Finding a place of ministry and serving there will be a valuable part of preparation. If there is an opportunity, a place in your local church may be available. Community ministries, from nursing homes to street ministries, may be an option. A more productive route would be to introduce yourself and ask for guidance from local pastors, denominational workers and local ministry leaders. You will need a helpful attractive resume to leave with them. You are likely to have friends and co-workers who are in churches outside your network. The scriptures tell us *"you have not because you ask not."* Ask God to guide you, friends to support you, and church leaders to use you. Your biggest enemy to success in finding your place of ministry is discouragement. After your first big effort of "marketing" yourself, and you see no results, you may want to quit. Don't quit, but you should rest, rethink what you have done, see where there is any possibility of help to return to and build yourself a second plan. Become intentional in your schedule, take your time in every occasion, enrich the friendships you have and don't stop!

While we speak of God's call in terms of your life vocation or bi-vocation, we also speak of the call of a church for you to be their pastor. While an opportunity may involve a lot of human activity, the final word is God's. This is the place God has prepared for you to serve and wants you to be their pastor.

The human activity is also guided by God, or the process will fail. It is important that you make yourself known as a candidate for pastor. To do this, you will need an attractive resume. The best resume is not necessarily the most attractive, nor the shortest or the longest. Think of the resume as the way you want to be introduced to church leaders, fellow pastors and denominational leaders. My resume begins by stating my life mission. If you have not developed a concise three sentence mission statement that would be a good exercise in describing yourself. Your resume should have your name, address, phone number and e-mail address. You have the choice of listing first your experience, your education or your honors/recognitions. Perhaps you chose to put the one with the most helpful information about you first. If you have valid experience, I would suggest you put that first. If in your educational organizations one of them gave you specific training that would be of interest to a church, list that with the school. Another section can be any awards, honors or recognitions you have received.

Other than your experience and education, the most important part of your resume is your references. Some resumes I have seen state that references will be provided upon request. You can't afford to do that. Your references may be the place where you may attract attention from a seeking church. I urge you to enlist people personally who will allow you to list them as references.

If possible, you will need to list persons whose names will be recognized by churches where you share your resume. Make an appointment and visit these persons, tell them about yourself and answer any questions they have. Your best introduction to them is your Christian life story, experiences you have had and what goals or life mission you have. I personally prefer a picture of you, or you and your wife, on the resume. If you do that, always make sure the pictures will copy well. Make sure your copies are very clear and on quality paper. Any resumes you mail out, prepare a warm personal letter to accompany them.

With your resume in hand, visit all the persons you think can help you. When you call for an appointment, ask for an appointment of approximately 15 minutes to ask for the person's help. Your list of visits should include Directors of Missions, Superintendents and pastors in the area where you want to serve, church leaders and mission leaders. Ask all of these in your visit if they know of a church seeking a pastor. If so, get as much information as possible including the contact person for the search committee. Ask the person telling you about the church if they would consider sending that church your resume with a personal letter. As you do these visits, carefully build a list of possible churches with the contact information. Pastor searches often have times of excited possibilities and times of dead end streets. Do not give up, trust God to guide you. Make yourself available to be a supply preacher or prayer meeting Bible Study Teacher. These activities will open doors for meetings with key leaders and search committees. In these meetings, be prepared to use the format mentioned two paragraphs back and plan to be knowledgeable and interested about the church. Remember, this process is part of the "search process," both for the church and you. Try not to be anxious, but prayerful. In your search about the church, determine what is the regular dress style for Sunday services and dress to fit that style. Look sharp and be sharp, regardless of your interest.

The process, as you may know, is for committees or committee leadership to meet with you, determine if there is a sense of God's blessings on you serving there, invite you to preach what is often called a "Trial Sermon" and wait to determine the intention of the church. Many churches require a congregational vote to call a new pastor. Although there are mitigating circumstances that could change this number, a vote of 60% or more is best to judge the will of the congregation. By this time the financial conditions have been worked out and discussed by the congregation. You then have the opportunity to respond to the invitation of the church, assuming that the vote is positive. Unless you have prayerfully arrived at a response, you have the opportunity to take your time in shaping your decision. It is always best that you have an enthusiastic "yes" before you announce your decision or you are comfortable with all concerns. Don't feel you must answer quickly. When you give a positive acceptance of the call, do so with a whole-hearted attitude. Like marriage, you are accepting the people and the church at large "for better, for worse."

The most important element of the decision is that you believe deeply that God has called you to serve that church. The elements we discussed in your personal call to ministry earlier in this chapter are reliable in interpreting this call. Those elements, a sense of oughtness, growing enthusiasm and a confirming experience, can be used to arrive at your answer.

How you begin a new ministry is an important part of that ministry. Some begin very quietly, showing up and preaching on their first Sunday. If you are a quiet person, that may be your most comfortable way to begin. You will need to take your church in consideration as you make suggestions about this occasion. Your considerations could be: Does the church need some positive news to celebrate? Does the church need to get the attention of the community? Does the church need an occasion to reach out to inactive members? If so, plan an "Installation Service." There are several models of these available in pastor's resources. You will be wise to put your ideas in the hands of a committee or leadership group and let them claim the credit for the day's success.

Finding Your Footing and Your Voice. You have done many things that require good footing and good voice. If you have played sports like baseball, golf or tennis, you know that it requires a good footing to hit the ball. You cannot swing hard at a ball when your footing is slippery. In ministry we must establish good footing, something firm to stand on. Where do you find stability and a firm foundation? May I mention a few and ask you to add to the list?

Your Christian experience of salvation: This is not just what happened "when you were saved." These are the things you have done and continue to do to strengthen your relationship with Christ every day.

Your continuing relationship with Christ: This is the need for a consistent love and obedient relationship with Christ every day.

Your passion for your calling: You have been selected, invited and prepared to represent Jesus. Keep the focus on representing Him, not projecting yourself.

You have opportunities to serve "the least of these" and the affirmation you sense as you serve.

Your Christian community, fellow ministers, friendships and family. Christian ministry and living is a shared experience. You can't do it alone. You need others and they need you.

But there is a vital second part of this challenge. *You must find your voice.* You may build a strong foundation but be unable to speak the word God wants you to say. I'm not talking about volume of speech, loud shouts or quantity of many words, but your true message from God as you minister to others.

While we often try, we cannot borrow another's words. Some minister's words are always what they have read or heard lately, not what God's word is for the day. Your *voice*, God's word channeled through you, comes from your heart, life and spirit that God has under control. It is always in development within you each day.

Perhaps it would help to identify how our voice is developed. Let's explore the *sources of motivation and passion.* Emotions are a powerful force, especially in ministry. The caution is that many other strands of emotion seep into our mind and heart. We have personal convictions and prejudices that flow into this voice source. *A second source is our knowledge,* understandings and convictions. God uses the streams of intellect and reason to shape our voice. Finally, *we all have unique temperaments,* creating challenges with self-control and moods. Consider what a cluster of resources that feeds our voice!

Now, if I haven't lost you, let me sum this up. As we minister, we mature in both finding our footing and finding our voice. Those who are veterans like me remember seasons of ministry where we had poor footing and a weak voice. Of course, one of the ways we compensated was to preach louder and faster. I have come to believe a chief way the Holy Spirit works in our ministries is to put us on a firm footing and put His message in our mouth. We live in an ocean of words – conversations, television, phones, etc. We often feel we are drowning in the sea of words. When we truly speak for God, when our words come from God's weaving of His passion, mind and self-control, people will know it is the voice of God.

Larnell Harris sings two songs that speak to me deeply. His song, "Were it not for Grace" reminds me of how God has shaped my life. The second, "When God Calls," describes in majestic words the blessing of His call on my life. Reflect on his description of God's call.

† When God calls we stand before the maker of the universe,

† When God calls He lifts our spirit far from all the realms of earth,

† We tremble at His bidding, with our feet on holy ground,

† A consecrated summons to the throne room of His power,

† We bow and worship Him alone, when God calls.

RECOMMENDED RESOURCES
FOR THIS CHAPTER

Bickers, Dennis W. (2004). *The Bivocational Pastor:* Beacon Hill Press.

Dale, Robert D. (1998). *Leadership For A Changing Church:* Abingdon Press.

Hammett, Edward H. (2000). *Making The Church Work:* Smyth & Helwis.

SERMON RESOURCE

Stand Up for Jesus
Acts 25:23-27; 26:1-8; 24-29

In the opening chapter of the Book of Acts, Jesus gave this assignment to His disciples, *"You shall be my witnesses"* (Acts 1:8). He knew that unless they did become witness of the gospel, His life, death and resurrection would be in vain and Christianity would be dead. That is why he also gave them his presence, the Holy Spirit, to help them accomplish their mission. Had they not have been successful; we would not be meeting today. Today the assignment is still the same and the danger also the same. We who are believers and followers of Christ have an assignment and a powerful ally. We are to be His witnesses and we have His spirit, the Holy Spirit, to guide and empower us. Like the first disciples, the gospel of Jesus is just a generation away from extinction. Instead, the Book of Acts, originally named the Acts of the Apostles, is the story of regular people, out of ordinary lives, whose names are recorded in the best selling, most popular book of all ages, fulfilling that assignment. In our scripture reading today, the last major event is a dramatic witness to the most powerful two persons in that part of the known world. Before we see how this story unfolds, let's look at the cast of characters.

† Festus was the new governor of the area. He has just assumed the position from Felix, perhaps the most selfish and cruel ruler of that country. Felix only held his position because his wife was a daughter of King Agrippa I. Festus was 70 years old and would die soon after this event.

† King Agrippa II, the last ruler from the family of Herod the Great, was a Jew. Because of his family's ruling relationship to Israel, he boasted of being an expert on Jewish affairs, especially to the Romans. He had brought his wife, his half sister Bernice.

† Paul was to appeal his case in a hearing, not a trial, for he had already appealed for justice to Caesar, ruler of all Rome. For the governor and king, they heard him to determine what they would write

to Rome about his charges. For Paul, this was the opportunity God had promised him at his Damascus road conversion, saying he would preach to kings.

From these scriptures, we will examine how we are to be witnesses. Not that one of us will expect to witness to royalty; except that our goal is to help others become a "child of the king." However, there are some qualities that we can intentionally develop in order to be an effective witness for Jesus. The first characteristic we must develop is "a prepared life", an essential part of our witness. How many times have we tried to help people memorize scriptures and learn the right phrase in order for them to be a witness, but it never worked. A church was seeking a new pastor and someone asked one of the leaders what kind of preacher they were looking for. He replied, "We are not looking for a person with a prepared sermon but for a prepared person who can preach a sermon." The Apostle Paul was a prepared man. He was born in Tarsus, making him a Roman citizen. He was born into a Jewish family, making him a Jew. He was educated by the best teachers, became a noted scholar of the Old Testament, earned the title of Pharisee and expressed his leadership role by hunting down and killing followers of Christ. His conversion was dramatic enough to stop his aggressive spirit and turn his drive into serving Jesus. God had given him the assignment of being the first missionary to the Gentiles, about 99% of the world's population. He had spent two years preparing for this witnessing opportunity. From his jail cell he planned the event as a boxer would his next fight. His life's entire journey was invested in this witnessing appointment. It was for him a "Divine Appointment" and Paul knew that the Holy Spirit, God in the present tense, would be his coach and guide. He was not intimidated, fearful or negative by the event. Our lives also prepare us to witness to those we meet. We are all different in how we approach the opportunity, and we have different life experiences from which to draw. I usually want to know something about the person and when possible, find a place where we have something in common. This allows me to use what God has taught me in the conversation. We all have places God has prepared in our lives that we can share with others, even when those places are mistakes and transgressions. Paul began his witness by identifying with his hearers, especially King Agrippa. Paul's heart always went out to those in his race and tradition. In his missionary visits to new cities, he would always visit the local synagogue. When Festus told him, "You are free to talk," Paul was ready. He could have condemned King Agrippa for his immoral life, but he did not. He appealed to Agrippa as a Jew from birth, one who knew the scriptures, and one whose family had been involved in Israel's political life for decades. He also noted that Agrippa saw himself as an expert in Jewish affairs. Our witnessing opportunities are not provided for us to discuss sports, politics or the weather. We are there to address a person's spiritual life, something that today's culture sees as very, very personal and private. You may want to begin by asking the person about their spiritual journey or how they feel about a specific, but not controversial, spiritual subject. In Evangelism Explosion, we were taught to ask a person, "If God were to ask you, 'why would I let you in my heaven', what would you say? Before we can begin to introduce Jesus as Savior, we must listen for the needs to be met. Paul's central theme was his testimony. After all, a witness is someone who tells what they have seen or heard. Our testimony is uniquely our story. You may be like me, becoming a Christian in a very quiet way as a child. However, my testimony is about the blessing of my life with Jesus is to contrast to what my life could have been. Paul reviewed his journey through the Jewish steps to leadership, his zeal to persecute Christians and his dramatic moment of meeting God on the Damascus Road. He insisted that he has remained true to the prophets of Israel, who Agrippa knew about. Paul's climatic statement was that Jesus, who died a criminal's death and was buried, rose from the grave and spoke to Paul in his conversion experience. Both rulers knew of many religious persons, even notable leaders, who had been crucified during their time in leadership. None of them knew of anyone who had been raised from the dead. This is where the witness event stopped. Their response was quick and negative. Festus called Paul crazy, saying "his great learning had driven him mad." Agrippa was more subtle. His familiar statement, *"Almost you persuade me to be a Christian,"* (Acts 26:28) may have been his intent. However, more recent translations point out the word used means "a little," which could say "a little more and I could believe." Some translate this statement to read, "Do you think you could convert me this way?" Paul's answer was a classic. With no apology or rebuke, he considered himself their peer and said, "I want you to be like me, except these chains." Paul knew he served the king of kings, and all other kings and powerful persons received their role from God. He also knew they needed what he had and that the world would be so much better if they were followers of Jesus. Paul invited them to be a follower of Jesus. The story is told of a meeting of students and friends at the University Of Chicago Divinity School. The program was a well-known visiting professor who spent his time quoting scholars about religious philosophies. When questioning time came, an older man stood with a question. He was eating an apple as he spoke and asked the professor, "Do you know how this apple tastes?" The professor rebuked the man by saying, "Of course not. I would need to eat the apple to know that." The older man gently responded, "That's true, and I don't think you have tasted the Jesus I know." The psalmist invites us to "taste and see if the Lord is good." Jesus invites us to come, follow me and I will make you …" Paul's prayer was that these powerful men would meet Jesus and taste the gospel He has provided. Our invitation is that you will say "yes, I will", not "almost, but not quite."

[CHURCH]

REPEATING YESTERDAY OR
MOVING TO TOMORROW

CHAPTER THREE:

SERVING CHRIST THROUGH HIS CHURCH

*"I will build my church and the gates
of hell shall not overcome it."*

MATTHEW 16:18

After 2000 years of being man-handled by so many millions of persons, members, leaders, critics and enemies, the church has not only survived, but also thrived. It carries the high claim of being the "body of Christ" and the burden of being led and occupied by sinful persons like you and I.

The church has been manipulated by governments, world leaders, corporate powers, political shame and evil leadership. The church has survived power struggles from within and outside world forces. There is hope for the church.

For us who follow Jesus, the church is our spiritual

family, containing our supporters in times of trouble, our allies in times of conflict, and our identity. Just as God chose to create His identity with the nation Israel and the human person Jesus, He now has placed His human identity in the church. Scriptures dare to call those early believers, one generation away from heathenism, the "body of Christ."

That's who we are! Both that big church downtown and that little church located on a dead-end road in a rural area are "the body of Christ." A study of the churches described in the New Testament will show you a realistic picture of churches that are not a pretty sight. Yet it is in the backdrop of all these scenes that Jesus said, *"I will build my church and the gates of hell shall not prevail against it"* (Matthew 16:18). When we look at the history of the church between the first New Testament churches and today's churches, we are amazed where the church is now. We wonder where the church will be after the end of this century?

Perhaps you haven't seen all of that in the church where you are. You may see a small building, a smaller crowd, limitations in ministry and opportunity, and discount where you are. It is very easy to describe why you cannot accomplish your dreams in a place like that.

In the world of small churches, there are two basic mental attitudes existing among churches. Most small churches are looking back at yesterday, talking about what happened in the past that was good for them or what inflicted the fatal wound on them. These live in the world of "yesterday," are comfortable there and cannot recognize any possibilities of looking forward. Their most forward look is next Sunday or next holiday celebration. Having only a view of yesterday makes their present tense very discouraging.

There are pastors of small churches who choose to live toward tomorrow. They embrace hope of tomorrow through their faith in the living, ever-present Christ. This sense of faith and hope releases the creativity of the Holy Spirit to work among them. It allows them to see possibilities, not obstacles. It helps them create ways to minister beyond "we've never done it that way before." After all, the sign-off phrases of the smaller churches are either, "we've never done it that way before," or "we tried that and it didn't work." As a bivocational pastor, you will choose the kind of ministry you want to pursue. It's very safe and comfortable to settle for a traditional ministry, preach well, endear yourself to the people, try not to lead in bold ventures and just "keep on keeping on." One of the first decisions you will make, either intentionally or by default, will be if you will lead your church toward tomorrow or settle for yesterday's style of ministry.

SERVING AS A BIVOCATIONAL PASTOR

Characteristics

There are some common characteristics you will need to study as you consider being a bivocational pastor of a specific church.

Understand your Church

† *Each church will have a set of beliefs* and, while they may not match up exactly like yours, they serve as a base of central beliefs for the membership. In our day of diversity, it is not essential that everyone who signs on believes all of these. People choose to come into a church for a number of reasons, such as location, family ties, friendships, style of worship and ministries offered. While these beliefs are part of the core principles of the church, the bivocational pastor will find it more fruitful to focus on ministries and fellowship to grow a healthy church.

† *Every church will have members and leaders.* The bivocational pastor will find learning about this area and connecting with the people is the first order of business. Each person and family unit will have their own story of how they came to be members and leaders. Often it is helpful to sit down with two to three long-term members and go over the list of persons to get early information before

you connect with each person. You will be seeking to learn not just people and their jobs, but also the present level of commitment these persons bring to membership and leadership in the church. The effective bivocational pastor will always be looking for ways to raise this level of commitment throughout the church.

† *Each church has a meeting place.* As the bivocational pastor, you will want to think about what the location, building and grounds tell you and the community about the church. What do these say to the outsiders who see them? Often the members and leaders do not see the facilities as the outsiders do.

† Except for new church plants, *each church has some experiences with a pastor/preacher.* Most churches, in their years of existence, have had a succession of pastors. A review of these pastors' ministries will give you a good history of the church. A church's personality or culture is usually shaped by the leadership you will follow. That includes both the pastors and lay leaders of the church.

† *Every church has a format for doing ministry,* often called their ministry program. Every piece of that plan has a history. Most of it has been imposed by

denominational input. The key question in this area review is, "Does this plan fit the present and future needs of the church and its' world or did they only fit the yesterday of the church?" With the current condition and resources of the church, how should the church be ministering today?

† *Each church has a budget, or spending plan,* for the offerings being received. This area is of vital importance for the bivocational pastor, not to supervise, but to understand and keep in focus. In the Watergate investigations in our nation, the one sentence that helped investigators solve the crime was "Follow the money." That is true of many areas of business and life, including the church. It is a key area of power in the church also. What we call budget is the "spending plan." This is constructed by a deliberate process of planning and church approval or informal, accumulative process of "that's what we always do." The very practice of handling money can be a positive thing that everyone feels comfortable with or a negative thing where there is a power struggle. Trust is a key component of this process. As bivocational pastor, and possibly moderator of church business meetings, your attention to this area is very important. The rule of thumb is expressed in the advice on how to handle

a raw egg - "not too lightly, not too tightly!"

† *Every church has a level of fellowship* among members and as bivocational pastor you will want to be very careful in quietly and quickly learning about this. Most churches have some history in disagreements, even as severe as church splits. Most churches carry some wounds and some scars. Quite honestly, with as many areas of diversity and possible disagreements, it is a major miracle that churches function as well as they do. As bivocational pastor your role will always be on the side of maintaining fellowship in the spirit of Christ.

† *Every church has a future,* a positive or negative chapter of ministry being written as you serve. I am convinced that every church can have a positive future if they choose to allow the spirit of Christ to reign. As bivocational pastor, your central message must be the need and benefits of allowing the head of the church, Christ, to lead and rule within the church. A friend of mine went through a period of time in his ministry of severe illness that left him disabled. During that time the church he had served as a seminary student in Kentucky contacted him about returning there to serve as their pastor. He felt so inadequate. He could not speak well, his

body strength was low and his confidence depleted. Not knowing if he could do it, he accepted the call with one condition - that they would move forward only as they truly felt it was God's will. Returning to this church, located next door to a distillery in Frankfort, Kentucky, he and the church faithfully kept the covenant they had made. Soon the church was overflowing in attendance, new buildings were being built and today that church is a dominant church among Kentucky Baptist churches. My friend has moved on to his next assignment in Mississippi, healthy and always excited about what God can do. This is an excellent model for ministry in smaller churches.

Of these eight characteristics of smaller churches, some of them merit more attention. Within a smaller congregation, two areas have the most potential for misunderstanding or growth.

The first of these is the commonly held beliefs of a church. In my church family of Southern Baptist, we have broad disagreement over a document called *Baptist Faith and Order,* a statement of faith and practice. In recent years the denominational leaders have led in adopting new versions of the document to address specific areas of disagreement, and to strengthen the beliefs of current leaders. Most of our smaller churches are not informed or interested in which version is correct. Within the same denomination there is disagreement about Calvinism and a list of social issues. At the same time there are prospective members coming to churches seeking one of two positions. Many come seeking to find a conservative position where specific beliefs matter very much as they look for a church home.

On the other hand many come seeking a church where there is broad agreement on traditional Christian beliefs, and they seek a church that is very accepting and inclusive of persons who have a wide variety of attitudes and opinions about many of these beliefs. There is always the damage that one or more leaders may force agreement on some of these beliefs and create a fellowship issue.

The second area of potential discord is within the area of personal relationships. It would be interesting to draw a web indicating relationship connections within a small church. There are kinships, long-term friendships, and church-related relationships such as committees or leadership positions. Those can be distorted by decisions made by the church, issues from outside the church or family issues. These are on-going possibilities and can have lasting impact.

The wise bivocational pastor is loving and understanding, but not involved in the conflicts unless the welfare of the church is involved.

The bivocational pastor faces two major challenges in relationships to the church. His largest challenge is with the current congregation, those who attend, support and see themselves as most committed to the church. Within this group are the leaders, the long-term members, faithful workers and attendees. If your ministry is to be effective, these are to be your traveling partners. Their first loyalty is usually to their church and to you if you are helpful to the church. They are the ones you must convince first on any plans to move the church forward. There will be in that group key leaders who can help you move forward, but you must explain and ask for their help. Your faithful services as their pastor are essential to win their support. That will be especially true in major health crisis, death and other pastoral opportunities.

The second challenge will be to create a spirit of optimism within that group about the welfare and future of the church. One way this can happen is to reach out to those who have dropped out of attendance. Many of these will rediscover their need of the church and the relationships that are offered.

Often you will find yourself the pastor of a small group of senior and mid-life adults with very few children or teenagers. While the long-term solution is complicated, it may be possible to reach and energize some younger families with children. Young adults can bring major resources to your church, including a livelier atmosphere, giving, leadership potential and added growth from the friends of these families. My wife and I have had success in reaching young adult families by conducting a marriage and family workshop and launching a new young adult Sunday School class. Having a children's time in worship is also a positive activity. Such initiatives are strengthened by enlisting two or three young adults in the church to help you.

I understand the smaller churches today do not put their best foot forward and are not without blame. In these days of fast transitions, churches cover the landscape of our nation, and often remind us of yesterday. I believe God is at work in His churches. While many, if not most churches we see, do not live up to the ideal I speak of, I believe God is at work in every church in some way, depending on the freedom given Him by that church, and each makes some contribution to His kingdom work.

I believe serving Jesus through the church can give significant meaning to our lives; a quality Jesus called "abundant living." My life was shaped by Jesus through His church. As a young farm boy, I accepted Christ and was baptized into a small country church with a bivocational pastor. As a teenager, I responded to God's call into ministry and my pastor took me to a Christian college and said, "This is Jimmy. He wants to become a preacher. Help him all you can." In my second year at college, a small suffering church called me as pastor. They had thirty three pastors in the previous thirty years. By the time I was a seminary student and pastor of the church, the church burned to the ground on a Sunday. I was a candidate to a large bivocational pastorate a few miles away. Our Director of Missions persuaded me to stay and guided me as I led that church to move from the old location, on a dead-end road, to a location on a main highway. God helped me finish college in six semesters and summer school, and to do the same at seminary. Since that time, twenty-five years as pastor of a church and twenty-five years as a church consultant, God has richly blessed every chapter of my life. In my "third half" of ministry and seventy seven years of life, I have found that my commitment to Christ and to His body, the church, have been the source of great blessings in my life. I have learned that you make your life choices, and your choices make you. No wonder Jesus asked of His disciples, *"Follow me, and I will make you to become ....."* (Mark 1:17).

I believe the only things restricting churches are the lack of commitment, creativity and confidence in God!

You and I have the opportunity to help churches discover their best future and engage in the journey to go there. Join me in the adventure.

Several years ago the British Broadcasting Corporation was filming the life of street people in London, following them each day, recording their conversations and taking good notes. Back in the studios they returned to view their film. One elderly man pushing his grocery cart fascinated them. As he pushed his way through the day, he seemed to be mumbling the same words over and over. They had a microphone on his clothing so they turned the volume up to catch his words. With the static of the high volume, he was heard to be saying, "Jesus never failed me yet, Jesus never failed me yet." I think we can also say that of our own pilgrimage.

RECOMMENDED RESOURCES
FOR THIS CHAPTER

Hammett, Edward H. (2000). *Making The Church Work:* Smyth & Helwis.

Malphurs, Aubrey (1993). *Pouring New Wine Into Old Wineskins:* Baker Books.

McNeal, Reggie (2009). *The Present Future:* Jossey-Bass Publishers.

Schaller, Lyle E. (1991). *Create Your Own Future:* Abingdon Press.

Wood, Gene, Miller, Kimberly & Becker, Julie (2001). *Leading Turnaround Churches:* Churchsmart

SERMON RESOURCES

In the Meantime

JEREMIAH 29:1-14

All of us have stored in our mind favorite scripture quotations. We often pull them out to quote on an appropriate occasion. That may be called Biblical "cherry picking." Seldom do we look at the larger passage from which the quote is found.

Today's scripture passage is the context from which we look at a familiar favorite promise. *"I know the plans I have for you,"* declares the Lord. *"Plans to prosper you and not to harm you, plans to give you hope and a future."* (Jeremiah 29:11) We quote these words to help people be encouraged, focus on the future and give God the credit.

A look at the preceding verses, the context of that statement, shows us another picture of trusting God. The people receiving this promise were not very encouraged. More than six hundred years before Christ, the Israelite people had been conquered by the nation Babylonia. King Nebuchadnezzar had led his army to defeat their nation, destroy Jerusalem's walls and houses and take back to his country those citizens most useful to him - craftsmen, teachers, musicians, and key leaders and even the king and queen. He marched them to Babylon as slaves. They were forced to adjust to being slaves, find a place to live and take care of their families, captives in a foreign land, humbled and discouraged.

In the early years they dreamed of going home. Their prophets and fortune tellers told them their stay in Babylon would be short. Only God's true prophet would tell them the truth. Jeremiah was left in their native land, consoling those left behind. He wrote a letter to the exiled remnant of his people to tell them the truth. "They are captives of things they cannot change."

We have our own story and offer our best excuses. We are often captive of what we can't change. It may be our health, jobs or careers, finances and debts, marriage

SERVING AS A BIVOCATIONAL PASTOR

and family, our faith and our failure. Jeremiah told them how to handle this "in the meantime" chapter of their nation's history.

† *Face the Facts.* Jeremiah tells them they must come to terms with their circumstances (Jeremiah 29:1, 9-10a). Here are the facts – they are exile slaves, and will be for 70 years. They cannot change that. He also told them that the voices that they are hearing were not of God. These were false prophets, wanting to please people. They were leading people to have false expectations of the future. They were not sent as a messenger of God. They must face reality. Their generation will die in Babylon. The only hope for contributing to the future of their nation will be through their children and grandchildren. Scott Peck, a Christian psychiatrist, spoke about the dangers of avoiding reality. He called that "the beginning of mental illness." Jeremiah coached them on living in this "meantime" period of their country.

† In Psalm 137, the writer tells about their attitudes during this period in Babylon. They wept because as slaves, their masters insisted that they sing the songs of their homeland. Their question was this. "How do we sing the Lord's song in a strange land?" In their resignation they chose to hang their

harps on the trees and stopped singing! There are times when each of us wants to give up, lay down and quit.

† ***Don't Put Your Lives on Hold*** (Jeremiah 29:4-7). Their future would not be fulfilled in their lifetime. They would marry, build their homes, and raise a garden. They were told to keep on living. There is a popular Christian song that encourages us to think about "until then." Their best contributions in their life will be living for the future of their nation. Building family is a way of building a good foundation for our nation also.

Live in a space called "in the meantime." "In the meantime" pray for and seek peace in the strange land they found themselves in. It could not be the contribution that kings and leaders dreamed of making, but it was something they could do. As a pastor, I have walked with some gifted and committed Christians through the gates of a prison where they would spend the next chapter of their life. They chose to study the scriptures, witness to other in-mates, hold Bible studies when possible and walked away a blessed person.

A stranger instruction is this, pray for peace and prosperity of Babylonia, their place of prison. The benefit of this is that the slaves will prosper also. That peace and prosperity will not come by listening to the false prophets. "Until then," keep on praying and working in peace.

Reinhold Niebuhr wrote this prayer: "O God, grant us the serenity to accept what we cannot change, the courage to change what can be changed, and the wisdom to know the difference."

† *Hear and Believe the Truth about God!* God's truth included accepting the facts of their exile and slavery that the exile would last 70 years, so get on with living their lives. But there is more. They were told that God is faithful. He will come and lead them back to their Promised Land. We who live on this side of the cross and resurrection of Jesus know His promise, *"I will never leave you or forsake you"* and "Nothing shall separate us from God's love."

Jeremiah came to present one of God's greatest promises for these slaves when He promised, *"I know the plans I have for you," declares the Lord, "Plans to prosper you and not to harm you, plans to give you a hope and a future."* (Jeremiah 29:11)

That promise is as true today as 600 years ago. 630 years later, Jesus began a new kingdom, a new presence and new power.

We may be "captives of what we cannot change," but Jesus came to set us free. We have a future, a hope, a home. Jesus came saying, *"Follow me, and I will make you become.... fishers of men"* (Mark 1:17). Our hope and that of so many others is fulfilled as we live and tell about Jesus.

[PREACHER]

THE WITNESS OF THE GOSPEL AND THE CHALLENGE OF MINISTRY

CHAPTER FOUR:

THE BIVOCATIONAL PREACHER

*"It pleased God by the foolishness of
preaching to save those who believe."*

I CORINTHIANS 1:21

If you have been in vocational ministry very long, no doubt you have heard the generic name for the pastor, "preacher." I've often wanted to react by calling the person addressing me as "preacher" by his occupation: plumber, nurse, carpenter, farmer, etc. I kid the person that, when their church changes pastors, there is no need to learn a new name. Just call the new pastor "preacher." I also remind people that being the preacher is only one of several hats I wear, like counselor, administrator, shepherd and leader. Perhaps that comes because preaching is the most public part of my ministry.

It is true that we have overused the ministry of preaching in most of our churches. If we have three worship services, it is easy to have the pastor preach three times. Often I felt like I was drowning in an ocean of words, most of them mine. Preaching is the primary way we choose a pastor, even if his gifts may be better in many other ways. Our preaching forms an initial perception of us in a church. After you have been with the church for some time, people will remember you not by a specific sermon, but by a specific ministry act in a time of great need in people's lives. In serving smaller churches as bivocational pastor, the preaching ministry will be the main way we can bring leadership, counsel, Biblical instruction and evangelism to the church body.

Bob Dale, in his book *"Leadership for a Changing Church,"* identifies the pastor as the "meaning-maker" for the congregation. This was the primary teaching style of Jesus. A "meaning-maker" seeks to make sense of events in people's lives, the confusion in a changing culture, rules that are changing and choices that must be addressed.

The Apostle Paul identifies another motivation for preaching is evangelism. In Romans 10:14-15, he argues, "How can they call on the one they have not believed in? And how can they believe in the one of whom they have not heard? And how can they hear without someone preaching to them? And how can they preach unless they are sent?" That is not to say that every sermon must be an evangelistic sermon. In fact the preacher as a "meaning-maker" will always have a wide variety of preaching subjects ready to be addressed.

Your preaching ministry must be the central responsibility you engage in for your church. It is the area where you can have regular direct communication with your people, address any area of church life that needs attention, insert any level of encouragement needed by your people and do so on a very personal level. Your preaching becomes your way to evangelize lost persons, coach Christians toward growth and service, and underscore any area of concern you have both for your church, the community and the nation. It is the opportunity for you to teach the essential ingredients of our faith and urge Christians to engage in the practice of witnessing, giving, prayer and fellowship. Let's talk about how you enhance your preaching ministry in your church.

First this test, in Frank Pollard's book, "*The Preaching Pastor,*" he asks us to consider five essential questions about the preaching ministry.

   † *Have you bought what you are selling?* Are you a committed follower of Jesus? Is your relationship with Jesus up to date? Do you think more about Him or yourself as you minister? Are you transparently in love with Jesus?

† *Can you do without it?* Is the claim or call on your life for real? If you can walk away from it, rethink your commitment. What things, personal desires or destructive habits are in your life that could destroy you?

† *Is the main thing the main thing?* Is Jesus very real and current with you? Do you serve with passion or habit? Are you excited to lead someone to Jesus and help them grow?

† *Are you real?* What are you like when you are all alone? What shortcuts in the practice of your faith appeals to you? Are you consistently humble about yourself and proud of Jesus?

† *Who is in charge of your career?* Do your career goals honor Jesus? Are you confident God will take care of you? Do you trust your family to the abundant care of God?

Did you pass the test? If so, let's move on. If not, stop and settle these questions in yourself.

Your experience of God's calling on your life and your response of gratitude and a willing heart will foster several building blocks that will undergird an effective preaching ministry.

† Your sense of the presence of Jesus, alive and lead-

ing in your life, an up-to-the moment relationship with Jesus Christ is the wellspring from which your ministry flows. It is your responsibility to have the desire to be connected with Jesus and the time to invest in this relationship.

† Your experience of living by faith, demonstrated by your acceptance of God's call on your life, will give balance to your life. Your faith, enriched through prayer and service, gives you confidence to love others, listen to the guidance of the Holy Spirit and to obey the direction of God in your life.

† You will practice discipleship of thought and life. Your consistent pattern of Bible study and prayer becomes the foundation of learning and practice essential to relevant preaching.

† Your sermons are ultimately tested and improved in the context of fellowship with others. Fellowship with your fellow Christians strengthens your ability to express your message. Fellowship with those not yet believers increases your passion to communicate the gospel.

Preparing to Preach a Sermon

Let's look at the process of preparing one sermon.

A church-planter pastor told me of a gigantic discovery he made in his ministry. He worked for three months to gather his first congregation and to preach his first sermon. He had worked almost every day on his sermon. As he concluded that first Sunday service, he realized the next sermon was due in seven days. This section is not meant to be a homiletics course but an outline of the process to be ready to preach one sermon. You will diversify your own. Just make sure you avoid any shortcuts just to get the job done.

Your preparation for the next sermon should include the following considerations:

† *The context of the sermon:* Who will hear it? Christians only or off-the-street homeless persons? What type of worship experience will be needed to match the sermon? Where will the service be held?

† *The study for the sermon:* Choose your topic and/ or scriptures for your sermon. Study and pray until you have the conviction that your choice is God's choice. Examine the Scripture with a creative mind. Look at it from several angles. Begin to build the framework, the theme and the outline, of the sermon. Read what others have said about this scripture. Consider your life experiences and past Bible study thoughts.

† When I entered the parallel ministry of fund raising for churches, I took a leave of absence from the preaching ministry for 25 years except for three to four well developed sermons used in my capital campaigns. I also began to give away all of my books except for two sets of bookshelves containing my favorites and some classics. When I returned to preaching as a supply or interim preacher, I discovered the rich resources on the internet. I consistently used Sermon Central, both for commentary on a selected scripture or subject. I have also contributed some of my better sermons there. I recommend that you browse Sermon Central and look up sermons posted there.

† *Construct the sermon* in a way you can follow. I am an "outliner" and need an outline for many things I do. Others build a set of words, phrases or scripture from which to speak. Consider writing it out, not to read but to develop the vocabulary of the sermon. This is your final preparation step before you preach, so build it in a way that helps you remember the message.

† *Preach the sermon:* Consider how you are most comfortable with your body stance, your voice, and your mannerisms. Consider the flow of your

sermon and the tone and volume of your voice. Let the Holy Spirit, the Spirit of Jesus, speak through you!

† *Before you preach again* develop a system to file your sermons then move on beyond the past sermon. Consider how you want to adjust the process of preparation. Take a day off from sermon preparation.

The Role of the Holy Spirit

While we all accept the need for the Holy Spirit, God's Spirit, to guide and bless sermon preparation and presentation, we cannot assume that to be a reality. The Holy Spirit lives within us, given to us the day we received Jesus and is constantly active in our lives. In such areas of study and preparation, I find I pause a few minutes throughout the study time to open myself to His reflections. I am always amazed at the creativity and clarity the Holy Spirit brings to me in those times. Also when I lay aside my study for a period, the Holy Spirit continues to work in my mind to help me.

Worship Planning

Any worship is made better by planning. If you serve in a ministry similar to me, planning time is the hardest time to find. With a volunteer music leader, and all of us on tight schedules, I have been able to have a brief worship planning time once a month, usually Sunday afternoon. This has helped our music group and I feel like we are on the same page, discuss the areas where we have felt God truly leading us and admitting that sometimes we have missed His guidance. We have also developed themes for each month and a better sense of fellowship as we work together. I recommend that you try this, regardless the size of your church

Funeral Sermons

We who preach have several different opportunities to conduct funerals. Some of these are our closest friends, church members and family members. While some of them may be emotionally stressful, we have great confidence in the fact that this person is already with God. We are asked to conduct the funeral for some persons we know, but not well. We will need to take the time to learn more about these persons. Sometimes we are asked to conduct a funeral of a stranger. This may happen when a member of the family, the funeral director or a third party recommends you.

The content of a funeral sermon has three purposes to fulfill, and you may even shape your sermon around these purposes.

† ***You are there to honor a life.*** Everyone deserves attention to the important thing in their lives and the impact one life can make. In this way you can honor a great saint or call on the audience to remember the good in the person's life. Always show credibility in your remarks.

† ***You are there to comfort those that mourn.*** We don't all grieve the same way, but we all grieve. Recognizing that you understand grief is important.

† ***You are there to honor Christ,*** share the good news of His death and resurrection, and help people open their lives now to Him while they still live.

You will find many scriptures with which you can craft a helpful message to the family and friends.

When you conduct a funeral, always file the sermon, the person's name, family members and date in an orderly way. Be careful not to preach the same sermon without changes for several families.

RECOMMENDED RESOURCES
FOR THIS CHAPTER

Anderson, Leith (1998). *Dying For Change:* Bethany House.

Hawkins, O. S. (2006). *The Pastor's Primer:* Guidestone.

Mims, Gene (2003). *The Kingdom Focused Church:* Bethany House.

Pollard, Frank (2003). *The Preaching Pastor: Publisher Not* Available.

Wood, Gene, Miller, Kimberly & Becker, Julie (2001). *Leading Turnaround Churches:*   Churchsmart

SERMON RESOURCE

When We Get Stuck
ACTS 11:24; ACTS 11:18-26

If you've lived for a few years, you have experienced being stuck – sometimes by physical circumstances, sometimes by emotional obstacles, sometimes by career issues like job/boss, sometimes by family problems.

The Bible is a wonderful, "real life" book for our life. It shows where multiple people and nations get stuck and how they either go under or go forward. Before we get to the focus passage, let's review some situations of how God's people can get stuck. The story of the nation

Israel is the key focus of the Old Testament. It is a story of starts and stops, wanderings and marches, good leaders and bad.

Joshua's story is one of my favorite. This nation had been led by Moses out of slavery, delivered by the Red Sea miracle, began the march of over a million people across a wilderness. They had stops and starts, high moments and horrible moments until they came to the edge of their Promised Land. There they discovered that their promised land must be fought for. There were insurmountable obstacles and they found themselves defeated before they tried. *They doomed themselves to be stuck* in a wilderness for forty years, only a day's journey from the Promised Land,

They built a temporary city for a million people and lived out their lives stuck, wandering in a wilderness on the edge of their promised land. Moses died, and with him that generation of people who voted "no" to go fight for their land. *They were stuck.* Only two leaders survived, Caleb and Joshua, who was the chief captain for Moses. Joshua was anointed by God to lead them and was ordered to "speak to the people, that they move forward."

After the nation captured and occupied the land, they began the process of *being stuck again.* They avoided their allegiance to God, married among the native, pagan people and became a leaderless, godless nation. God tried to provide leaders through judges and prophets, all locally based in the larger land, but the people desired a king and army like all the other nations that raided their land. *They were stuck.*

God chose David to be their king after Saul was a gigantic failure. He led them to shape the nation that would rule of the world. Solomon tried to maintain their greatness but at his death *the nation was stuck.* Like typical Baptist they split, divided into two weak nations, suffered defeats by neighboring nations and became a conquered land. *They were stuck.*

In His strongest move yet, God sent His son, Jesus. He was God in the flesh, God's true representative, and He began a new kingdom. He taught eternal principles of God, showed the love and power of God in His miracles, and trained twelve very ordinary, common persons to be his next generation of leaders. His death, burial and resurrection formed the life-changing experience that persons could claim as their salvation experience. In His last hours on earth He charged His followers, then and now, with His mission orders and gave them the power of His sustaining spirit. His spirit, coming in power on the celebration of the Jewish Pentecost, launched the church we now are a part of. His spirit delivered that person, and us, from *our stuck places.*

Wouldn't you know it! They began to *move to their next stuck place.* They quickly became the church for people just like them, the Jewish Christian Church that was going to exist only within their country's borders. God began very quickly to challenge their narrow-minded boundaries. Persecution drove them out of their country into other countries and they told of Jesus.

God raised up a key leader in a man named Barnabas. A new, quiet follower of Jesus, a man of Greek descent, who saw a larger world and more possibilities than others, saw. Two very brief scriptures introduce him to us.

Acts 4:35-37 [35] *and laid them at the apostles' feet; and they distributed to each as anyone had need.* [36] *And Joses who was also named Barnabas by the apostles (which is translated Son of Encouragement), a Levite of the country of Cyprus,* [37] *having land, sold it, and brought the money and laid it at the apostles' feet.*

As the Christian movement grew larger, it became more cautious. The apostles, disciples of Jesus, leading the church became Jerusalem centered and accepted their issues of dealing with the Jewish leaders. The Christian community was discriminated against and many were forced into poverty. The church began receiving offerings to help them and Barnabas felt the need to give as did many others. However, Barnabas did more. Having property, a rare possession for a Christian and possibly his only claim to financial security, he sold his property and gave it to this need. No wonder he was renamed "Barnabas, Encourager.

Here we see that Barnabas was Sold Out for Jesus: We are by our human nature accumulators. Whether it is land, cars, titles, awards or friends, they become our signs of security and pride. Jesus asks us to not *get stuck* about these things when He taught, "Where your treasure is, so will be your heart." Your heart does follow your treasures. "Give and it will be given unto you, pressed down and overflowing". Barnabas chose to invest in Christ's kingdom and others. Giving, a big part of stewardship is how we function as trustees of all God have given us. One of the places we practice this is in our churches. Often we think that others will do that. We park on their nickel. It has been said, "God loves a cheerful giver, but receives from a grouch."

Acts 11:19-26 [19] *Now those who were scattered after the persecution that arose over Stephen traveled as far as Phoenicia, Cyprus, and Antioch, preaching the word to no one but the Jews only.* [20] *But some of them were men from Cyprus and Cyrene, who, when they had come to Antioch, spoke to the Hellenists, preaching the Lord Jesus.* [21] *And the hand of the Lord was with them, and a great number believed and turned to the Lord. [22] Then news of these things came to the ears of the church in Jerusalem, and they sent out Barnabas to go as far as Antioch. [23] When he came and had seen the grace of God, he was glad, and encouraged them all that with purpose of heart they should continue with the Lord. [24] For he was a good man, full of the Holy Spirit and of faith. And a great many people were added to the Lord. [25] Then Barnabas departed for Tarsus to seek Saul. [26] And when he had found him, he brought him to Antioch. So it was that for a whole year they assembled with the church and taught a great many people. And the disciples were first called Christians in Antioch.*

Barnabas is described as a "Good Man." Barnabas became the first Christian friend that the apostle Paul had after his conversion. Barnabas brought him into the leadership of the church in Jerusalem and supported him as he tried to achieve acceptance. When that was not to be, Paul retreated to his home area of Tarsus. Barnabas continued quietly and faithfully within the Jerusalem church. When the Christians in Antioch began to receive Gentile Christians into their fellowship, a new step to world missions, the church chose him to go see what was happening. He went to Tarsus, brought Paul into the ministry, and was a co-leader of the church. Paul quickly rose to be the key leader and

Barnabas willingly took the lesser role.

Barnabas was humble. He had no need to be first. He was not working to be noticed or the key leader. He was serving Jesus, and all he did demonstrated that.

Barnabas was a visionary. Quickly projecting hope, he saw the big picture of God's plans and joined Him there. He crossed boundaries of race, culture and old thinking to help the Antioch church grow even before Paul came.

Barnabas was unselfish. Because he had no need to be leader of leaders, he rejoiced in the success of Paul and moved from the key leader to one of five key leaders to serve in the church. Later when Paul objected to taking Mark on the next journey, Barnabas took Mark on a separate trip and developed him to be the inspired writer of the first gospel about Jesus. Barnabas never sought prominence, but a way to serve Jesus.

Barnabas was full of the Holy Spirit. The driving force of that early group of Christians was not their wealth, education or political clout. It was the Holy Spirit, the spirit of Christ at work in the lives of regular people. The Holy Spirit directed the events on that stage, prompted those who spoke and brought the right audience to see and hear the message. It was the Holy Spirit, the spirit of Christ, that launched and advanced the church. Barnabas, from his seat in the group but not the dictator of the dictator, demonstrated what God can do with a quiet, unassuming person sold out for Jesus.

Barnabas was full of faith. In the marriage program called "Five Love Languages," there is identified a love tank that we all have. It is either full or empty, depending on the investments of our spouse, family and friends. Perhaps we also have a *faith tank.* One person describes faith as "believing what ain't" but the Bible describes faith as *"the substance of things hoped for, the evidence of things not seen."* (Hebrews 11:1)

Faith gives us that physically invisible sense of confidence we have about the future and our role in it. It is important to notice that Barnabas is described as full of the Holy Spirit and faith. They are companion qualities that make our Christian life work. To have the Holy Spirit but nowhere demonstrate it doesn't work. To have faith without the personal power of the Holy Spirit is a dead end street. Barnabas was empowered by the Holy Spirit to move forward in faith.

Where do these things fit in our personal world? Are you stuck? Isn't that your choice to be stuck? When we decide to give our full allegiance to Jesus, to sell out to Him, we can have opportunities to move forward.

Is your church stuck? Does this quote fit your church? "They do it every Sunday, they will be okay by Monday, and it's just a little habit they've acquired."

What role do you and I play in getting our church to "move forward?" Are we helping the church move forward with our attitudes and efforts? Are we part of the problem, or the answer? Helping or hurting?

Churches are by nature cautious, conserving organizations. We are holders of the faith, believing and fighting to be sure the message is conserved. Often we stop there, get stuck there.

God's expectation of our church is that we will move on! We are called to leave behind yesterday, with both its valleys and victories, and move in faith into the future. God is already out there, waiting for us to join Him.

The difference between Christianity and any other world religion is this. We follow and serve a risen Savior, while all other religions learn and try to follow a dead leader, He still calls us out of our stuck places with *"Arise, go. I will be with you!"*

[PASTOR]

SHEPHERD OF THE CHURCH BODY AND
HELP FOR PERSONAL JOURNEYS

CHAPTER FIVE:

THE BIVOCATIONAL PREACHER AS PASTOR

"It was He who gave some to be ... pastors ... to prepare God's people for the work of service so that the church may be built up until we all reach unity in the faith and in the knowledge of the Son of God and become mature, attaining to the whole measure of the fullness of Christ."

Ephesians 4:11

There was a time when someone acknowledged a call to minister, it was assumed that the person would serve as preaching pastor. Today there is a wide range of ministries blessed by God and included in His call. There are ministry roles of chaplain, minister to youth, missionary and many more ways to live out our calling. In fact, many of us will serve in several ministry roles before God takes us home. This chapter is for those who are seeking to understand the minister's pastoral role with the congregation. It is perhaps the most demanding in time, the most demanding emotionally and the most draining spiritually. It is also the most rewarding in personal relationships, the most enjoyable socially and offers the longest tenure of the largest number of friendships than other ministry roles.

Pastoral Care is Provided in Many Ways by the Bivocational Pastor

To the majority of the church, it occurs Sunday by Sunday at church. Taking your time to have brief, but relaxed conversation with people can be very meaningful. One or two questions about themselves and their family demonstrates that you understand their needs.

In some of those contacts, persons will have more serious needs as the recent loss of a loved one, a recent illness, divorce, financial crisis, or a child away in school, all requiring you to request an update from them. When possible, pause for a brief prayer with the person wherever you are. This can happen in the hallway, at the exiting line and in a pew when greeting people.

Many times a member will ask for a meeting to discuss a problem or opportunity in their lives. You have the option of deciding when it can fit into your schedule.

Often a pastoral visit is conducted in a hospital

where the pastor goes to see the person as a patient and parishioner.

There are some helpful reminders for you, as you prepare to visit in one of these settings.

† Keep in mind who you represent. You are there to represent God, your church and fellow Christians.

† Be careful to see your conversation as considered confidential by you and hopefully others who are present. Often an "off-hand" remark is heard in a critical way, though you did not mean to come over as critical.

† Keep the visit discussion on the person you are visiting. Although the person may want to know about yourself and others, be careful not to give out personal information.

† Make your visit brief, but memorable. If possible find a way to sit down. If there is a need you can meet for the persons, volunteer to do so.

† Plan to have a time of scripture reading and prayer as you conclude. Keep the scripture verse and prayer short. Make a graceful exit as soon as you can.

Pastor care is the most time consuming, and both as tiring and rewarding, as any part of the pastor's life.

To define it, let's say that it is providing personal attention and support in both the usual days of life and the crisis times of life. Because of the limitations of time and energy for the bivocational pastor, this area of ministry often gets the short end of the pastor's time or causes you to neglect other important areas. With the demands of preaching, administration, crisis occasions, evangelism and our own personal time budget, the on-going contact with those in the congregation and community needing a visit, a prayer or an encouraging word, may feel neglected. I suggest that you begin with each church or your new chapter in your present church, with a major pastoral care initiative.

A major reason for the absence of personal home visits is not just the lack of available time, but the changing living patterns of families. The home is now considered a private retreat, not a gathering place. This major trend is called *Cocooning*. The home is now seen as our private retreat place. Many of us go home, push the garage door opener to enter the door, push the opener to shut it down. It's as if we have entered into our old European castle, surrounded by a mote, which is filled with alligators. When someone close to us wants to come for a visit, we let down the draw-bridge, open the garage door and welcome them. Otherwise, we live cocooning in our private space. A second reason for not being visited is the limited time a bivocational pastor has to arrange an appointment. Our members are as busy as our bivocational pastor and finding the best time to visit is very hard. There are no times in most homes for a drop-in-visit.

Let's assume that you have been called as pastor in a very valid process in the church and received the majority vote from the members. Because first impressions are the most lasting impressions, you will need to plan with church leaders your first Sunday and the first month of ministry. Your leaders may want to have a dedication moment in the service with prayer for you as you serve as pastor. The women may want to have a welcome lunch after the service to begin making connections between you and the members. You may want to choose your clothing more carefully, press them more thoroughly and make sure you and your family looks your best. This is the first day of your new pastorate!

The best way to start a new pastorate is to get very busy very soon. As a bivocational pastor you have limited time to give each week. For the first week mark a calendar with your "on the field" times reserved. Your goals, even with your time constraints, are to meet as many members as possible away from the church. You remember them best by visiting in their homes, but that is becoming harder to do these days. One thing I have done is to enlist a few key leaders, deacons or Sunday School Leaders, to pick a time in your calendar, pick 3-4 names of member families, and take you to their homes. You should stay no longer than 30 minutes in each home. Determine some things you can learn that will help you know them. Ask these in the form of gentle questions and let them direct your conversation. When those are asked or time is up, ask if they have any questions, have prayer with them and conclude the visit. If you have a business card, bulletin or contact information, leave it with them.

Questions you might use to learn to know them are these?

- † How long have you been a part of the church?

- † If recently, what brought you to the church?

- † If children, ask for their names, ages, school and special interests?

- † You probably will want to inquire about their jobs, or if retired, previous jobs.

- † What is it you like best about the church?

- † What would you like to see happen at your church?

- † Explore other areas of friendship, previous locations, health issues and serious prayer concerns.

Let your prayer include the names of the people, the prayer needs they have and bless their home.

At the end of this visitation blitz, you will still have some that were not contacted. Some needing time to be able to welcome you and a few who you discover have signed off on attending your church. Commit yourself to loving all the people, preaching with warmth and conviction and always thanking everyone for their participation. You can also offer to be their pastor, regardless of their church affiliation. If they accept, be as faithful to them as you are to your faithful members.

Pastoral Events

There are some important personal events that bind a pastor to his people - weddings, funerals and baby dedications. When performed in the spirit of love and servanthood, the pastor endears himself to persons and families and has his best chance to call people to a closer relationship with God. These three events represent key factors of life - marriage, family and the ending of life on this earth. Many times as a pastor I have found myself visiting with a young family in the hospital as they welcome their new child, and then go to another floor to visit with a family as their loved one passes. Developing your own approach to each of these will endear you to each family.

The Wedding

When you feel qualified and comfortable to provide counseling with the couple, you should schedule a structured visit with them. If you do not feel qualified to provide the marriage counseling, please urge them to meet with a qualified Christian counselor for this important preparation.

Your wedding preparation meeting with the couple should be the time when you learn to know them better and all the details of the wedding, so take good notes. Draw out the wedding platform plan on a pad. Learn to know the names and roles of each participant. List all the preliminary activities before the wedding; music, usher instructions, parent's roles and seating. If the wedding is not in your church, have a good understanding of the layout. If there is a wedding consultant, have the duties of the consultant decided early. Never let anyone turn the arrival time into a decision making meeting.

Be very careful to explore every part of the actual service. Father giving the bride away, the rings, how to get up steps for ladies, and what will be done at each step. The giving of the rings and the ceremonial kiss need to be explained. Practice the exit to make for a smooth transition to a reception or travel to a new location. Make sure you complete the license information

THE BIVOCATIONAL PREACHER AS PASTOR

and signing while you still have the persons available to do so. Accept whatever gift is offered and on the next day write a note of thanks and appreciation for the honor of conducting their wedding. (A sample wedding service is enclosed.)

The Baby Dedication

Let's be very clear that this is not infant baptism and is primarily a service for the parents. Two passages of scripture fit this occasion. In I Samuel 1:27-28, Hannah presented her miracle son to the priest, declaring: *"I have lent him to the Lord."* In Luke 2:52, baby Jesus was taken to the temple to be dedicated. The service can be used to underscore the miracle of birth, the baby as a gift of God, the vital role of parents in raising a child and that God has a place for each child in His kingdom.

One of the ways I enjoyed using to symbolize the dedication and potential of the child is to present each set of parents a beautiful rose bud in a vase, emphasis on the beauty of the child and the potential to grow. While it is popular to have all babies of the past year dedicated on the same day, I have chosen to always do the dedication in the month of the birth. Often there were several children even when we had the service only once each month.

The Funeral

Pastoral care becomes very intense and important in the death of a member or a member's family. I would never refuse to serve as a pastor to any family regardless of their church affiliation or Christian commitment. Those days are the most fruitful in presenting the gospel of Christ to the family and their friends.

Usually the pastor is involved with the family before the death of their loved ones. In all the occasions of ministering to the terminally ill person and the family, there are many opportunities to present Christ as the Savior, the Comforter, the Sustainer and the one preparing a place for us in Heaven.

The pastor may be present at the death, in the funeral home with the family making arrangements and throughout the time of receiving friends and the burial. His presence reminds people to have confidence in God. At no time does the pastor take charge, but is open to the request of the family for times of scripture reading and prayer.

The funeral home usually has a format they use for funerals. Should you want to make changes, talk to the funeral home staff before you do the family. They can tell you if a specific format is the usual form or the one the family has requested. You will be asked to lead the graveside service. Often there will be one or more ministers assisting you or you are assisting them. It is appropriate that the deceased person's pastor bring the sermon. If there is a problem, ask for help from the funeral director.

Your role and participation will be made easier when you develop for yourself a Spirit-driven "theology of death." Time and experience with death, both in your life and in the lives you minister to, will help this development. Years ago I read a quote that I appreciated, and hope will be true of my life. A mother, praying for her son who was to be executed, called death, "a rest for broken things, too broken to mend." Most of the deaths I have experienced, both with my family and many others, are truly "a rest too broken to mend." When we are tired, broken whether physically or emotionally, God takes us home with Him and gives us rest. (Funeral resources are enclosed.)

Baptism

One of the greatest celebrations for the church is a baptismal service. Baptism is the time that a new Christian declares by action what Jesus has done for that person and their witness that they have trusted Jesus as their Savior. It is also a time of bonding with fellow Christians, doing the act just like they have. It becomes then the time the new Christian spiritually joins the church.

A baptismal service should be planned for the new

Christian as soon as possible, but with no sense of urgency after the public profession of faith. All of the readiness details should be cared for by fellow members. I chose to never plan the service as an "add-on," but do it very early in the service. In our church I meet with the candidate 30 minutes before the service and release them to get ready. While the congregation is singing an appropriate Hymn, like "O Happy Day," we enter the baptismal pool. I introduce each candidate and recognize their families before baptizing the person. I then ask the candidate if they have trusted Jesus as their personal Savior. After their answer, I make this pronouncement: "Upon your profession of faith, and in obedience to *His* command, I now baptize you in the name of the Father, the Son and the Holy Spirit." As they arise from the water, repeat this phrase: "You are buried with Christ in baptism; you arise to walk in newness of life."

They are helped out of the pool, instructed to get dressed and come into the worship service to sit with their families. Often I have their families sitting in the front pews of one section and speak to the candidates and families later in the service. We ask those baptized to stand at the front to be encouraged by the church body. (A sample baptismal sermon is enclosed.)

Lord's Supper

Just as baptism is a celebration of entrance into the church, the Lord's Supper is a celebration of the on-going fellowship of the Body of Christ as it remembers its roots and continuing mission. No doubt you have been a part of the Lord's Supper service many times. While the gospels tell the story of the Last Supper with Jesus, Paul's instructions in I Corinthians 12:23-26 help us understand why and how to continue the practice of the Lord's Supper. This is one of those times when your leaders are well trained to serve the supper. Your role will be to lead the service in a meaningful way.

Like the act of Baptism, I do not ever tack the Lord's Supper onto the regular worship service. I feel it will mean less to the people, not be appreciated, because it will add 20 minutes or more for time conscious wor-shippers and often cause we who lead to rush instead of reflectively guide the service. Most often I plan the service to lead up to the Lord's Supper, give a 10-15 minute sermon on some aspect of the meaning of the celebration, lead the Lord's Supper and close with an invitation to make a personal, if not public, decision. I encourage churches to conduct the Lord's Supper bi-monthly instead of quarterly.

Ordination Services

Your church can conduct two different ordination

services, one for your church's new deacons and one for ordination of ministers. The ordination of deacons is very much a local church event, although other churches may choose to be involved. As the pastor of the church and the leader of this service, you should research the way your church has conducted deacon ordinations in the past. How they selected the deacons and received church approval. How they have planned the service and convened an Ordination Council. When has the service been held and what was the format of the service as well as how the candidates were affirmed and recognized.

The basic difference in ordination of a candidate for the gospel ministry is that the candidate is being ordained for the wider ministry with other churches and the area churches are invited and urged to participate. The ordination council will be made up of ministers and deacons from other churches as well as yours. Most important, this service launching a career for the candidate entitles the candidate to certain honors and benefits that are significant and establishes the candidate as a model for Christianity. Any negative behavior will not only embarrass your church, but Christianity at large. It is no wonder that Paul advised Timothy, *"Do not lay hands on anyone hastily."* I Timothy 5:22

Church Business Meetings

There are those times when it will take all the personal skills and spiritual understanding to conduct or participate in a church business meeting. Most small churches elect the pastor to be their moderator. My view is that, while this is often an uncomfortable position, I would rather be able to guide the meeting than try to speak to an issue as a voting member. More churches have been divided; members offended and ministry weakened by poorly guided business meetings.

My advice is to learn to use Robert's Rules of Order very skillfully. Know what is on the formal and informal agenda, keep the meeting moving forward and do not allow for free time for gripes. Use your authority with kindness and with no favoritism to anyone. Stay in touch with the mood of the group, as some will want to dominate the meeting, and keep firm control at all times.

Connecting With Denominations, Associations and Conventions

While many churches will not be connected to a larger group of churches, such as conventions and associations, most churches will have some relationship with groups of churches similar to them. As a pastor, you will benefit from meaningful participation with other churches. Being pastor can be a lonely life and pastors need peer relationships where they can share more freely. In most areas of church life, groups have regular pastor's conferences, annual conventions and places to find helpful resources. There are helpful organizations outside of your group that can provide education, leadership resources, services to meet personal and family needs and guidance. I urge you to explore who these resource groups are and how they can be helpful. After the initial educational and supportive resources you have received, it will be your personal responsibility to connect with these good people to continue the personal development and learning journey for your career.

Pastoral Counseling

You will become a "go to" person for many persons dealing with personal and family issues. In most cases these are far beyond the ability and time you can offer these persons with needs. Your best plan is to have one listening session with them and then refer them to a reputable Christian Counselor. I have a book to recommend to you written by my wife, Dr. Patsy Highland, entitled *Marriage Counseling 101: A Practical Guide for Ministers*, that is sold on Amazon.com. She will help you sort out what is being said and where to go with it. I want to warn you about assuming you can help many people. The area of mental and emotional health has many challenges and the pastor can do much damage while trying to be helpful. Often a person who turns to their pastor for help exposes some very private part of their life and leaves the church when they consider what the pastor knows. Sometimes the pastor gets dragged into family and legal controversies which is harmful to them personally and to the church. My advice is, love them, pray for them, be cautious with advice and refer them to a professional counselor. You will need a list of reputable counselors, received from your fellow pastors or area church leaders.

Political Issues

I don't need to tell you that our nation, your area and your church are rigidly divided on most political issues. Some of these political groups claim to have spiritual purposes and as well, national well-being. My basic boundary is simple. Political forces try to use the church influence and voters to accomplish their primary purposes. Those purposes are political power that brings advantage to a chosen few. In the past decade we have seen all political forces, not just one side, turn their skillful forces on churches to accomplish their goals, not the churches goals. Pastors, whose influence should never be bought, must declare their church a "no politics zone" in keeping with the primary purposes of the church.

Concluding Thought

When Jesus sought out Simon Peter after His resurrection, He found Peter and other disciples on the banks of the Sea of Galilee where they were returning from a night of fruitless fishing. The leadership of the church that Jesus had planned was present that morning. Jesus began to question Peter about his commitment to the church and gave him his marching orders. The conversation went like this, Jesus: "Do you love me?" Peter: "Yes, Lord, you know I love you." Jesus: "Take care of my sheep." Those orders haven't changed, have they?

RECOMMENDED RESOURCES
FOR THIS CHAPTER

Bickers, Dennis W. (2004). *The Bivocational Pastor:* Beacon Hill Press.

Hawkins, O. S. (2006). *The Pastor's Primer:* Guidestone.

Macchia, Stephen A. (2003). *Becoming A Healthy Church:* Baker Books.

McIntosh, Gary L. (2002). *One Church, Four Generations:* Baker Books.

Smith, Fred & Goetz, David L. (1999). *Leading With Integrity:* Bethany House Publishers.

Steinke, Peter L. (2006). *How Your Church Family Works:* Alban Institute

SERMON RESOURCES

Sample Baptismal Service Message

This message was delivered in a baptismal service for several young persons. They were baptized early in the service and they were asked to return to the service as soon as possible. They sat in an upfront pew with their families behind them. The pastor came from the position on the floor level to talk to them and also to the entire congregation about the meaning of baptism.

READ MATTHEW 3:13-17

We are going to put your baptismal experience into a bigger picture and hopefully make for you a more memorable spiritual experience.

Jesus started His ministry by being baptized. As a young man He left His carpenter's shop and made His way to a baptismal service. For years He had worked as the village carpenter, but the time came He realized He had a much bigger life mission. Though He was born a human being, He was really the Son of God, sent to reveal God in a very specific way and to provide for all of us a way to be saved, live life abundantly and go to heaven when we die.

Today you have publicly started your place in God's kingdom. This baptism experience is your way to publicly witness your faith in Christ, your forgiveness of sin and your willingness to follow Jesus. When you place your faith in Jesus and decide to be a faithful follower of Christ, you testified to several important realities in your life.

† *You have asked Jesus to forgive your sins* and to continue to forgive as you ask Him to. He has done that and will continue to do that.

† *You have now received His spirit, the Holy Spirit,* to be a constant resident in your life. Your body is now the "temple of the Holy Spirit." He will work in your

mind to help you think His thoughts. He will work with your emotions to guide your feelings. He will direct your actions to guide you in serving Him.

† *God has a plan and purpose for your life* and He will empower you to find and live out that plan and purpose. He will never leave you or forsake you and, even if you try to exclude Him from your life, He will love you and call you to listen to Him.

† *He has promised to prepare a place in Heaven for you* so that where He is, we will be also.

Today you have joined a larger spiritual family called "church." Just like everyone in your family has a matching blood characteristic called DNA, you have a spiritual blood characteristic because we all are saved by the blood of Jesus. They welcome you into the family!

You have a home with your spiritual family. Some of us have been in the spiritual family called church for a long time. They want to help you as you grow in your spiritual life. All of us, including you, have a special place to serve and learn in this spiritual family. You will benefit from that only as you stay involved in this your church.

You will represent Jesus and His church from this day forward. What you do to help Jesus and your fellow family members will benefit us all. What you do that is wrong will hurt not only your spiritual family but also, Jesus. We will all be working to serve Jesus and to help build His Kingdom.

Today you have a new story - one that is uniquely yours. Jesus came to be baptized by John the Baptist not because He needed forgiveness, but because He was doing what God, His heavenly Father, had sent Him to do. He left the baptismal waters and entered into a wilderness to experience temptations that would shape how He would carry out His mission. You will experience some questions and testing to shape how you should fulfill your mission for Jesus.

The test is always, "How do I live out this commitment to Jesus?" I wear a ring on the third finger of my left hand that we call a marriage ring. On a specific day and in a specific place, I made a vow to "love and cherish" my wife, to be true "for better and for worse, in sickness and in health," and to be faithful to my wife. The minister told us, ""The ceremony is over, but your life of being faithful and loving is now beginning."

Church membership is a "need-meeting" relationship. We need each other and do what it takes to meet the needs of each other. Our relationship with Jesus is also a "need-meeting" journey. Jesus has no hands but ours, no feet but ours, no voice but ours. We have no enduring strength than His, no true forgiveness for our sins than His, no abundant life here and eternal life beyond this world than what He provides for us.

Sample Wedding Ceremony

Introduction

I want to assume we all remember I Cor. 13, and I believe we all can quote the last verse:

> *"And now abides faith, hope and love,*
> *and the greatest of these is Love."*

"Now there abides", = lives, abides among us,

Faith Abides Among You:

> Your experience with God in the past,
>
> gives you confidence at this time;

Hope Abides Among You:

You have a vision for your future together.

God gives a future and optimism about tomorrow.

Love Abides Among You:

You are surrounded by Love – your family,

friends and God.

Faith is built on our past experiences;

Hope anticipates our future experiences;

But Love is always present tense, something we experience, and express, each day.

Love is always a current affair, a "now' experience.

And the greatest of these. . .

Not Faith, though it steadies us;

Not Hope though it encourages us;

But <u>Love</u> – affection of your hearts and spirits.

Prayer

You are surrounded by those who love you, those who have taught you faith, and those who have great hope for you.

To Father

(<u>Bride</u>), your father is here to present you to (<u>Groom</u>), to represent your parents, and really all parents, in launching your future together. (<u>Father</u>), do you come to present (<u>Bride</u>) as the wife to (<u>Groom</u>), supporting her and (<u>Groom</u>) as they establish their life and home together?

To Groom

(<u>Groom</u>), do you Love (<u>Bride</u>) and choose her to be your wife? Do you promise to love her each day you live - in good times and in bad, in plenty or in want, in sickness and in health, and do you commit yourself to love her until you are parted by death? Do you promise this?

(I do.)

To Bride

(<u>Bride</u>), do you Love (<u>Groom</u>), and choose him to be your husband? Do you promise to love him each day you live - in good times and in bad, in plenty or in want, in sickness and in health, and do you commit yourself to

Love him until you are parted by death? Do you promise this?

(I do.)

Vows

Now join your hands, and speak from your heart these marriage vows:

> **Bride:** I, (Bride), love you, (Groom). I promise to be true to you above all others. I will stand by you, and do whatever it takes for us to share our lives together, with the help of God.
>
> **Groom:** I (Groom), Love you, (Bride). I promise to be true to you above all others. I will stand by you, and do whatever it takes for us to share our lives together, with the help of God.

Presentation of the Rings

Prayer

Now let's review what I Corinthians says about love, as we read the words from a modern translation:

> *Love never gives up.*
>
> *Love cares more for others than for self.*
>
> *Love doesn't want what it doesn't have.*
>
> *Love doesn't strut.*

Doesn't have a swelled head,
Doesn't force itself on others,
Isn't always "me first,"
Doesn't fly off the handle,
Doesn't keep score of the sins of others,
Doesn't revel when others grovel,
Takes pleasure in the flowering of truth,
Puts up with anything,
Trusts God always,
Always looks for the best,
Never looks back,
But keeps going to the end.

Conclusion

_____ and _____ we celebrate with you your love for each other, and recognize your commitment to each other.

It is not a ceremony that makes your marriage real. It is the honesty and sincerity by which you proceed to live out these vows.

Together, we proclaim that you are "husband and wife, and challenge you to live your love for each other daily.

You may kiss your bride.

[LEADER]

GUIDING CHURCHES AND INDIVIDUALS INTO THE FUTURE

CHAPTER SIX:

THE BIVOCATIONAL PREACHER AS LEADER

"A leader is not a person who can do the work better than others. He is a person who can get others to do the work better than he can."

FRED SMITH, SR.

It has only been a few years ago that I returned to the preaching ministry as a bivocational pastor. After I came as pastor of New Bethel Baptist Church, it was mentioned to me that they usually had an annual revival and it was time to schedule one. Not knowing many preachers in the area, I asked for suggestions. We settled on a man who worked at the Post Office and was bivocational pastor of a "First Baptist Church" in a small nearby community. I used our brief time together to ask him about his ministry as a bivocational pastor. He very quickly told me he gave no leadership to the church and it was not expected. He only preached and cared for those in illness or death. His sermons showed that, while he interpreted the scriptures very well, there was no appeal for moving forward in one's Christian life or the church. He chose a safe, comfortable role of preaching and pastoral care, but expected lay leaders to take care of the rest as they always had.

As we have said previously, every bivocational pastor has a choice of wanting to lead the church forward into tomorrow or accepting the role of maintaining the status quo for the church. Most members of smaller churches cannot imagine their church as any different than what it is now and would be concerned that any progressive movement would change things, thus upset some in the church and cause strife. The first Christian congregation in Jerusalem faced these issues and chose to stay in their comfort zone. Our churches, unless they are new church plants, are structured to rebuff growth for comfort. A girl sat in the balcony of her church, watched the usual service unfold and wrote, "They do it every Sunday. They'll be okay by Monday, it's just a little habit they've acquired."

But you would like to lead and you can! In a short story called "The Leader of the People" by John Steinbeck, there is a family containing an aging grandfather who had led wagon trains from the east to the west coast.

He told stories of his adventures, fighting Indians, wild animals and hunger. His grandson, Jodie, loved to hear these stories and begged his grandfather to tell them. Jodie's father, Carl, had heard the stories too many times and would try to stop them. When the story would end, the boy, Jodie, would say each time, "I'm going to be a leader of the people." His grandfather would say, "You can't be. We have reached the ocean edge and there is no place else to go." Jodie would reply, "In boats I can, in boats I can." We can all find our unique way to lead.

Styles of Leadership

Let's explore several different leadership styles we find in small churches with bivocational pastors. The *first is a negative style* I call "guess what I'm going to do next." This style is an impulsive approach, allowing the pastor to make decisions without consulting others. The *second style* is the benevolent dictator, using their position or experience to make themselves the resident expert. The *third style* is the collective consensus leader. This person asks anyone and everyone what should be done and enlists a number of leaders to name the next step to make.

There is model of effective leadership that we will name *"shared leadership,"* a process to determine what we can do together. Such leadership includes the understanding that leadership is a selfless act of service. It is not about self-gratification or acts of ego, but a servant heart. A second characteristic of *shared leadership* is embracing the Lordship of Christ. This includes the natural question, "Who is in charge here?" Lordship means the surrender of ourselves to the Lord Jesus and allow Him to lead us. *"Shared Leadership"* is also accepting "partnership" with others and with God to work as valued partners. The fourth characteristic of *"Shared Leadership"* is embracing a stewardship attitude. Stewardship, the reality of holding God's resources in our trust and accountable for their use, divides the responsibilities and the blessings of serving.

Now, let's move on from the philosophical to the practical. Every leader must have a foundation from which to begin. This foundation is both a guiding set of principles and a structure for people. The guiding set of principles will include your accepting the mission and values of your church. These principles have become quite popular among contemporary churches and can be found in print on most church websites. Sometimes the principles are called the purpose, the vision, strategy and administration. I prefer very simple, to the point, statements about mission and values.

A church I served in raising money for their ministry has three statements of mission. This state's what they want to accomplish as a church.

† To know Jesus Christ as Savior and to know the fellowship of His church;

† To grow disciples who live like Jesus;

† To go for Jesus into the world to share Good News and meet needs;

This is a good, clear, simple explanation of why that church exists. Too many words will just clutter and confuse.

The second part of their statement is the guiding priorities or values that will be honored in pursuit of the mission.

† People matter to God.

† Prayer is a priority.

† The Bible speaks to real life.

† This is a place of grace.

† What we do for God, we do well.

I am sure many of us will say this is too brief, too simple, and not spiritual enough. I have found that these values are easily accepted by un-churched people and simply state the attitude the church will embrace to do its mission. In my experience in working with small

SERVING AS A BIVOCATIONAL PASTOR

churches, the members cannot easily accept a grand vision of their best tomorrow as easily as knowing the main way their church should be ministering to be a good, healthy church.

The next step in leadership is to develop a simple strategy that the members can participate in together to achieve their mission. There must be a dozen proven strategies to organize and implement the mission. In 25 years of consultant ministry for building programs. I may have used many of these in some way. In the last 10 years of that ministry. I implemented a very successful structure of ministry teams that I recommend to you.

Team-based organizations can look and feel like anarchy. Time spent talking and brainstorming must be invested. Patience both by leaders and members is essential. Practicing respect and trust makes the strategy work and the church grow.

Leading the Leaders

As a bi-vocations pastor, you are probably looking at this strategy and saying, "When and how can I do all of this?" You can't, and if you are only doing what you can do, you are not doing enough! You also are not having much fun.

The key is delegation. The New Testament scriptures tell us that every church has within its congregation the resources to do its full ministry. As pastor, your first challenge is to become totally sold out on what this strategy will accomplish for your church. Your next challenge is to find the key persons to help you. You may need only about 4-5 persons to help you. Because this is your plan, with the purpose of helping their church, it may or may not need church authorization. It will take courage and confidence to launch this, but the rewards for you and your church are boundless. God's command to Joshua and many other leaders is "move forward."

Perhaps you've heard the story of a young preacher who approached the great evangelist D. L. Moody. The young ministry told Dr. Moody that he was a critic of how the great preacher did evangelism. He said Dr. Moody's style was too bold, harsh and insensitive to others. Dr. Moody heard him out and said, "You may be right. Tell me how you do evangelism." After several stuttering attempts to answer, the young man admitted he did not do evangelism. Dr. Moody replied, "I like my way of doing evangelism better than your way of not doing it."

Your place in keeping motivation and passion high in support of this plan is for you to be its best cheerleader. Leith Anderson, in his book, *"Leaders Who lead,"* suggests four things to keep doing. *One*, stay close to the action. This is no time to back away, be intimidated by critics or trust the process to maintain itself. In a small church, the pastor is the most influential champion of progress. Your team leaders and members must never feel you are not on the front lines with them. *Two*, your true authority to lead this effort comes from your followers. *Three*, plan to excel amid adversity. There are places where, in order to get past a tough place, you must stand with your key leaders. *Four,* sometimes you will need to take the initiative again to keep the momentum going. One of my opportunities like this was in the First Baptist Church in a county seat town in Appalachia. The town was the home of a decreasing number of millionaires, a growing Christian college and a dying First Baptist Church. The church building had been built primarily by the millionaire members during the Great Depression, but allowed to deteriorate during the next forty years. The building had never been updated or remodeled and was in bad repair. The young adults in the congregation wanted a renovated building and the older members opposed it. The church invited a building renovation company to do a study and present a proposal. In that business meeting the proposal was tabled by a Robert's Rules of Order deceptive move. The congregation left confused and defeated.

The next day a key leader came to the church to begin planning the new building program. He took the plans that had been presented and simplified them. He gathered local contractor prices and cut the cost in half. He presented his plans to the church and because of his sterling reputation and influence, it was approved. For the next six months he supervised the building program for the education and fellowship facilities and we dedicated the renewed building. As I thought over the dramatic change and progress of the church, I remembered the evening of the defeated proposal. After the meeting, I rode with him back to his house to lick our wounds. I tried to console him and he said, "Brother Jim, God has shown me this is something we must do, and we will."

There is nothing more powerful than a committed Christian with a passion to say and do what God wants him to do!

RECOMMENDED RESOURCES
FOR THIS CHAPTER

Barna, George (2001). *The Second Coming Of The Church:* Word Publishers.

Bickers, Dennis (2004). *The Bivocational Pastor:* Beacon Hill Press.

Cladis, George (1999). *Leading The Team-Based Church:* Jossey-Bass Publishers.

Hammett, Edward H. (2000). *Making The Church Work:* Smyth & Helwis.

Macchia, Stephen A. (2003). *Becoming A Healthy Church*: Baker Books.

McNeal, Reggie (2009). *The Present Future*: Jossey-Bass Publishers.

Rainer, Thom S. & Geiger, Eric (2006). *Simple Church*: Broadman & Holman.

Schaller, Lyle E. (1996). *The New Reformation*: Abingdon Press.

Smith, Fred (1986). *Learning To Lead*: Word Books.

Woods, C. Jeff (1996). *Congregational Megatrends*: The Alban Institute

OTHER RESOURCES

Why Do We Need A Team

The story is told of a church composed of Everybody, Anybody, Somebody and Nobody. Everybody knew a task had to be done, but was sure Anybody could do it. However, Anybody assumed Somebody would take care of it and as a result, Nobody did it. Everybody got upset and blamed Somebody, who pleaded ignorance and asserted that anybody should have been able to do it. Meanwhile, Anybody insisted it was Everybody's job. While those three kept on blaming each other, Nobody did what needed to be done. This is why a team is needed to accept responsibility for organizing, promoting and carrying out a successful stewardship program.

The most common reason for the failure of a plan is not that there was a problem with the plan. Plans fail because people fail to work them. People most often fail to do what appears too difficult or too unpleasant.

One key to making tasks easier and more pleasant is to help people work together effectively. Ecclesiastes 4:9-12 says:

> *"Two are better than one, because they*
> *have a good return for their work;*
>
> *If one falls down, his friend can help him up.*
>
> *But pity the man who falls and has*
> *no one to help him up!*
>
> *Also, if two lie down together, they will keep warm.*
>
> *But how can one keep warm alone?*
>
> *Though one may be overpowered,*
> *two can defend themselves.*
>
> *A cord of three strands is not quickly broken."*

This ancient wisdom tells us to avoid assigning a task to someone to do alone. Look for ways to have people interact on what they are doing. For example, while it seems efficient to say, "you call the people on your list and I'll call the people on mine," both callers would enjoy the task more if they could arrange to meet at the church and make their calls together.

Leaders should set aside time for prayer and for

building relationships before tackling the job. It is sad to think of Christians attacking a job together while never really getting to know or help each other in the process.

How to Launch Team Based Ministry

Have the basic questions answered before building the organization. Some questions to be ready to answer are:

† What are we trying to accomplish?

† What will this mean to our church when we are successful?

† What are the areas where a ministry team will be working?

† Is there a calendar?

† How will a team work to accomplish its purpose?

† How will a team be guided and connected to other teams?

Develop a plan to enlist and train team leadership. It is best to have the general leadership, often co-leaders, enlisted first.

† Meet with the church leaders to introduce the purpose and anticipated results.

† List the possible team areas of work and ministry. For example, if your purpose is to grow the effectiveness of key areas of ministry in your church, consider:

Prayer - Undergirding every part of this ministry growth in church-wide prayer

Outreach - Reaching out in the area around the church plus the network of persons connected to the church membership in specific acts of ministry

Every Member Care - Reaching into the membership of the church to provide specific acts of ministry to those in need

Community Ministries - Providing specific ministry opportunities to the community (holidays, community-wide events) and to specific group needs (single parents, senior adults, etc.)

Fellowship - Offering regular opportunities for member fellowship as a way to strengthen ties among members

† In a brainstorming session build a list of possible team assignments and list the names of persons that could fit that assignment. You may suggest a person's name in more than one place at this time.

† Enlist and train *team leaders.* Prepare written team assignments for each team defining the purpose, boundaries, possible suggested actions, and suggested size of the team and how to lead a team. When necessary, enlist co-leaders for larger orga-

nizational roles.

† Conduct a kick-off organizational meeting. Challenge team leaders to recruit for their team. Some team leaders will have all their team members in 24 hours and others will need help enlisting their team after this meeting. Have some suggestions ready for these persons. Everyone in the church, even those who serve as key church leaders, are candidates to be enlisted.

† For program, present the plan as clearly as possible and ask for questions. Then ask team leaders to introduce their team members. Finally, reserve the last 30 minutes for an initial team meeting.

† Next meeting, set a date to meet 2-3 weeks from this meeting. During this organizational period, meet every 2-3 weeks. After activities begin, meet once a month.

Maintain momentum by publicizing activities, recognizing ministry actions, testimonies of persons serving on teams and thank persons publicly.

The goal of this plan is to help your church function at its very highest level of ministry using lay leadership.

The Use of Ministry Teams

The basic unit of organization in this ministry expansion is the Ministry Team. A Ministry Team is a group of committed workers, specifically dedicated to working in one vital area of the ministry areas.

The leadership of this expansion is organized around core Ministry Teams. A core Ministry Team is a ministry area so vital that the expansion cannot be effective without it.

Each Ministry Team will be provided a Mission Statement, key dates that harmonize it with all other Ministry Teams, and some possible approaches to accomplish its mission.

However, all Ministry Teams will practice self-management. Within the framework of the team's Mission Statement and the campaigns key dates, the Ministry Teams plan and implement work in their area as the Team Members determine what will be most effective for their church. This self-management approach trusts people to know what is best for their church, encourages Team Members to "own" their ministry, and develops team players instead of "solo" workers.

Ministry Team networking is essential to the success of this expansion. The eight Ministry Teams must work together to create a unified effort. The role of Campaign Coordinators is primarily one of facilitating cooperation and networking among the teams. The Leadership

Team, composed of Campaign Coordinators and Team Leaders of each Ministry Team, is the best forum for correlating expansion progress. Ultimately, the key ingredient for effective networking is communication, and the best forum for communication is the Leadership Team and Ministry Teams.

Ministry Teams Leadership Plan

Ministry Teams are the most effective organizational approach to creating congregational involvement in ministry. Here are some proven reasons why Ministry Teams are most effective:

Ministry Teams have a single area of responsibility, providing them a clear Mission and Agenda even before they meet;

Ministry Teams are composed of persons who have a connection with each other and/or the ministry area;

Ministry Teams attract and utilize people who are action-oriented, team players and desire to contribute to the common cause of Kingdom growth;

Ministry Teams bring together the combined understanding, gifts and experience of its members to be invested in the accomplishment of a specific mission;

Ministry Teams when properly formed, trained and guided in the planning process, become a dynamic force in a successful venture;

Ministry Teams have members who consider their team membership, their meetings and activities a top priority in their personal lives;

What a Team Leader Does

Set times for team meeting and consider them sacred times. Contact your Team Members ensuring their presence;

† Keeps the focus on the Team Mission;

† Values and involves each Team Member;

† Collects and interprets the possible approaches to be used;

† Leads in decision-making for the best approach;

† Delegates and defines Team Members' roles/responsibilities;

† Maintains the time schedule for team activities;

† Affirms and recognizes work well done;

How To Lead Your Team

Set times for team meetings, and consider them sacred times. Contact your Team Members ensuring their presence;

Establish an agenda for each meeting, and what

should be accomplished;

Conduct the meeting in a way that involves everyone's participation;

Encourage adequate discussion;

Direct the team to acceptable decisions;

Determine who is to be responsible;

Set deadlines and next meeting date;

Keys To Building An Effective Team

Commitment - to the purpose of this expansion;

to the team mission;

to the team as a group;

Contribution - by practicing balanced participation;

by building synergy;

Communication - by listening;

by learning;

by deciding;

by planning;

by sharing with others;

Cooperation - by building partnerships;

by avoiding "solo" performances;

by creating cohesion in the team;

Coaching -   by clarifying the team mission;

exploring possible approaches;

by guiding the team to choose;

Coordination - by networking within the team;

by networking with other teams;

to teams as a group;

[WORKING WITH OTHERS]

SKILLS AND ATTITUDES FOR WIDER RELATIONSHIPS

Chapter 7:

THE BIVOCATIONAL PASTOR WORKING WITH OTHERS

I Thessalonians 5:12-15

When you agree with God and a congregation to be their pastor, you agree to accept the church "as is" and they agree to accept you "warts and all." The "as is" and "warts" will become known as you work together. You become a partner/leader/representative of God with a group of diverse persons. These are saints and sinners, leaders and followers, encouragers and detractors, cheerleaders and critics. Whether they could describe it, each has a role to play in your ministry.

This is to be a partnership in kingdom causes, and you inherit that kingdoms' mission and challenges. Your job is to work with as many as possible to accomplish as much as possible. We are going to examine "the others" in this partnership and then examine your part of the partnership. If I repeat myself from other chapters, it must have been important.

As we discussed, this group of persons in that congregation are the ones you will be working with. There are usually no star players to bring in or easy way to trade the negative voices for positives. This is your team. As we discussed in chapter four, *"Bivocational Minister as Pastor,"* a good start is essential for your success. My recommendation of every family visitation is the test I have to offer. Perhaps you've noticed that, in order for a rocket to get into orbit, it must start full blast and burn most of its' fuel to have a successful flight. It is important that you learn who the leaders are. There are usually both formal and informal leaders. You can discover from church documents who are the formal, elected leaders. Discovering the informal leaders will take more time and effort. Some of this comes into focus on your initial visitation plan.

In my experience of both being a pastor and being a consultant selling a building campaign, I subscribe to the belief that most smaller churches and some larger churches have a "nodder." This is usually a quieter man who has great influence. His influence may be that he is a leader of a large family, a person of above-average wealth, and an honored past leader or an honored public leader. Remember that power is always given to him by others and seldom grasped. An illustration of the "nodder" is this: the deacons are debating a decision to buy land for future expansion. Several deacons have been vocally for the purchase and two have been very vocal in opposition. As the time to vote is coming, many in the group are glancing at the quiet man in the corner. He has never said a word, but as the discussion has flowed, he has responded to some arguments by nodding affirmatively and to others negatively. While everyone knows how the vocal deacons will vote, the quiet ones have silently watched the older man, the "nodder," and vote with him.

Every church has a system of making decisions internally. It takes a big, controversial issue to force a public meeting and a vote. As pastor, it will benefit you to learn to know the informal leaders of your church. Some of them will be women who have taught a Sunday School class for a long tenure and/or been a mission's leader. Remember, in churches power is not grasped, but given. You can often begin to replace the formal and informal leadership. You can identify a younger or new member that you believe could fill that position and be accepted by the people. Then you can often mention the person as being capable, quote the person on some question or ask him or her to help present something that will be accepted.

Now, let's look at the need to sharpen your social skills. In my youth, (dark ages), one of the best-selling books was entitled *How to Win Friends and Influence People* by Dale Carnegie. The book created a business leader's training program and is still in business. That's a pretty good title for this section.

The best skill I recommend to you is the practice of listening. As "preachers," we live by speaking. Our supporters tells us what we have to say is very important. People listen to us, sometimes out of respect for our office, not us. The ancient formula is that we were born with two ears and one mouth, and we should listen twice as much as we speak. We all know persons, sometimes preachers, who talk incessantly for fear someone else will get the floor. We know people who are "word bullies," hitting on people with their tongue.

A good listener has these reasons to be quiet:

† Others have value and should be shown value by listening to them. Listening gives value to others.

† There is far more to learn than we have already received. Listening is a learning position.

† Listening helps us learn to know and evaluate others more precisely than any other method. The person's use of vocabulary, accent, slang and emotional force of speaking tells us volumes.

† Listening gives time to think, observe and decide our place in the discussion.

We also need to learn the power of "thank you." In my consultant role, I have often said that a "thank you" is the down payment on what I'm going to ask you to do next. The size of the thank you should be measured by the value of the gift. The gift of a compliment or another verbal gift can be appreciative with a verbal "thank you." The gift of a wrapped gift, dish or meal deserves a nice mailed note. More significant gifts deserve a more impressive thank you.

Another recommendation is to work hard on names and personal information for each member. Nothing is as appreciated as hearing their own name. You will gain instant appreciation as you call people by their names.

The Pastor's Friendships

Any chapter on your relationship as pastor should include a discussion of the pastor and friendships. At some point I remember a discussion about the dangers of friendships with people in the church. My life has been enriched, sometimes rescued, by friendships within the church. Besides, if we don't have friendships in the church, where do we go?

Nevertheless, I have these thoughts for you to consider. There are potential problems with friendships with some church members. There is an old saying, "Beware those who meet you at the train." In days when a pastor would take the train to a bivocational pastor position, a member would pick them up, provide room and meals and see to their comfort. Sometimes that person would elect himself to persuade the pastor. Therefore, the warning was "beware those who meet you at the train." I have personally experienced those people in my ministry.

Some of the most wonderful people you could meet are in your church. They want their pastor to be accessible and friendly. You will soon begin to gather in small groups for social occasions. You will be invited to eat with another couple or do something with another family. Often these turn into shared trips and vacations.

Your needs are very important. Our tendency is to isolate ourselves, fearful of occasions that are new to us. You and your spouse need a reliable support group, made up of persons you connect with. To discuss how a certain thing is done and who a specific person is, your wife may be your best radar detector. We need feedback on how we are doing and background materials on persons or events in the church. Most important, you need reliable contacts with the real world.

Two cautions are important.

† Do not form these friendships with a selfish person.

Often we link up to people who can help us at the moment, but hinder us later.

† Do not get into a friendship that is for another's selfish purpose.

† It is wise to understand that while you may choose a friend from the congregation, they also choose you. So discretion is advised.

RECOMMENDED RESOURCES
FOR THIS CHAPTER

Bandy, Thomas G. (1998). *Moving Off The Map:* Abingdon Press.

Dale, Robert D. (2004). *Keeping the Dream Alive:* Broadman Press.

Dorsett, Terry W. (2010). *Developing Leadership Teams In The Bivocational Church:* Crossbooks.

Hammett, Edward H. (2000). *Making The Church Work:* Smyth & Helwis

Mann, Alice (2000). *Can Our Church Live?:* Alban Institute.

Schaller, Lyle E. (1991). *Create Your Own Future:* Abingdon Press.

Steinke, Peter L. (2006). *How Your Church Family Works:* Alban Institute.

SERMON RESOURCES

Learning to be a Missionary

Acts 17:6; Acts 18:18

The writer Andy Andrews in his book "The Traveler's Gifts" sends his readers to seven different historical persons to receive lessons about life that he wants them to learn. You might want to read his book if you are seeking help in living life. We must all be lifetime learners, and there are those periods of time in which we must be intense learners. These may be the times when you first become a parent, you start a new career or you face a major health threat. Learning can be formal, as in a classroom or informal as experience on the job or supervised as in an internship. We are called to be "learners" of Jesus, even as those He called disciples. We often think of our spiritual heroes as not needing a learning period. I listened recently to Jim Henry, retired pastor of First Baptist Church of Orlando, Florida, and former president of the Southern Baptist Convention, tell of an experience in his first pastorate when a disgruntled member made a motion that he be fired. He spoke of what he learned from that experience. In my study of the book of Acts, seeking to find Lessons for Growing Christians, I was surprised to find see how Paul must learn to be a missionary on his first journeys... We picture him as the strong missionary leader, moving into the frontiers of pagan lands with the gospel. However, in the first journeys there are snapshots of learning opportunities for Paul. Paul, the Jewish scholar, former Pharisee, preacher, bold leader and Godly warrior, found that all of his training and experience, including his dramatic conversion experience on the Damascus Road, did not adequately prepare him to be our first world missionary. Even his brief time with Barnabas in Caesarea and on the first journey had not prepared him for this next trip. His first learning experience is found in Acts 17: 6-12, describing his time in Thessalonica. He was greeted with the pronouncement, "Those who have turned the world upside down have come here also." In his first two to three years as a missionary, he had earned that reputation. At least he was not guilty of bland-ness, dullness and passitivity. We can often be seen as dull and boring. Many people will not come to our churches saying that the services are boring; the songs are old fashioned and the commercial too long. Paul tried to speak to two very opposite audiences. In the synagogue he spoke to devout Jews who worshipped the yesterdays of Abraham, Isaac, Jacob and David. They practiced the same rituals their fathers had, heard the same readings and spoke the same chants. Paul came to tell them that The Messiah they had heard about all of their lives had come. The good news was that Jesus' death on the cross replaced the regular Temple sacri-fices for sin and faith in Him would bring them sal-vation. He also told of Christ's resurrection and the present power and presence of God today. Jewish lis-teners could not understand and embrace such a mes-sage to live in the present-tense presence and power of God. He was correctly accused of disturbing them so the religious leaders put him out of the synagogue. On the streets he met a new kind of audience. They were the working class pagans, always interested in a new god who could bring magic to their lives. When they heard about Paul's Savior who was crucified on a cross as a common criminal and resurrected, his good news story didn't fit their expectations. Their rulers turned on Paul as an enemy of Caesar's peace. There were a handful of new believers who helped Paul and Silas leave Thessalonica and journey to Beroea. As they walked that night to the next city, Paul may have pondered or discussed with Silas, "Why don't they understand?" This is the gospel, the good news. Why had his own people treated him so badly and the common man on the street would not honored him by listening? Change comes hard for a person or a congregation. Habits are firmly entrenched, old patterns are comforting and the practice of religion is only one small but important part of the average person's everyday life. The new is always hard to understand and easy to dismiss. It took a Damascus Road experience to bomb Paul out of his past life and thoughts. We who lead, teach and proclaim a new life in Christ still encounter huge obstacles. Even miserable people resist change, defeated people avoid being rescued and religious leaders still fear change. Thessalonica, like many of our places, was the community that valued sameness and routine and had a sign warning "Do Not Disturb." We have all been there/done that. If Thessalonica and even Beroea were the sleepy cities where change was not welcomed, Athens was obviously not that. In Acts 17: 13-34, Paul arrives in Athens as a lonely traveler. His companions remained behind in Beroea. It was a challenging place to be for Paul. It was the site for our second life learning experience. Athens was the intellectual capital of the known world. In the Greek world it was known for its scholars, philosophers, educational culture and its broad acceptance of ideas. It also had the largest collection of carved idols of pagan gods of any place in the known world. Perhaps Paul, in his idle times, waiting for his companions to join him, walked among the idols and read their inscriptions. He may have often sat in public places listening to the discussion of ideas and philosophies. As he waited he was disturbed by their pagan beliefs. He attended a local Jewish synagogue and discussed or disputed with the leaders their traditions and his faith. Interestingly, they were so passive they didn't put him out but tolerated his message. Athens was like that! As Paul roamed the city and discussed his faith with others, he became known as the source of a new religion. Because he was Jewish and a Roman citizen, he was invited to present his views to an elite group of scholars/philosophers that met at the Areopagus, their regular meeting place. Being an intellectual person, a trained scholar and an experienced debater, Paul found it challenging to meet with them. For the first time since his conversion, Paul chose to adjust his faith with a rational approach, build a bridge from where he was to where they were, and try to enter by the side or back door of their mind. He chose to compliment them for the religious expressions of the idols, and identify one statue to "The Unknown God" from which to introduce Jesus. The patient, abstract listeners were listening to him until he explained that Jesus died on a cross and was resurrected. He did not meet with anger, but laughter. This was beyond their rational thinking and philosophy to be humanly possible and could not be true. Most left mocking him and some considered hearing him again. There were those who became Christians but this was the place where many say Paul "flopped." There are those who compare Paul's writings in I Corinthians and say that Paul decided that in the future he would "only preach Jesus." We all have our places where we feel that we have failed. An executive search firm listed as one essential for their candidate "to have an acceptable number of failures". Like Paul, we may reflect on it and vow to never do that again. However, Paul would never again be in Athens and have the opportunity to share the gospel to the intellectually elite. He probably did his best. Our failures, like Paul's, must be viewed as a learning experience for us and as one small part of a fruitful life.

We cannot get stuck in our Athens, our place of mental gymnastics and philosophical discussions, and camp out among the proud few who want to disassemble the gospel to one thought-pattern among many. There are the "core beliefs" in our faith, certainties that give life stability and certainty that we must sustain. Paul's next learning experience (Acts 18:1-18) was in Corinth, one of the most evil cities of the Greek world. In contrast to the nice, quiet, rational environment of Athens, Corinth was known for two major economic realities, sailors and sex. Corinth was a major seaport city, complete with all the business related to it, the international population it brought there and the coarse lifestyles of the workers. Corinth was also the world center for the worship of Aphrodite, the goddess of fertility. The temples of Aphrodite were popular places, especially for men, because sexual activity was part of the religious experiences. The charms and ornaments about Aphrodite were made and sold by local craftsmen and were a major economic force. Into that world Paul came to experience a major, fulfilling learning experience. As he arrived he met Aquila and Priscilla, who became his life-long friends. Paul's journey to this point had been largely a solo flight. While he always had companions with him, he saw them often as "helpers," not peers. Aquila and Priscilla had become Christians before meeting Paul, so they saw him as a peer. They were from Rome where Paul had a great desire to visit. They were tent makers, as he was, and they had a home and a business where he joined them. Can you imagine their days a work, discussing their faith and their understanding of Jesus. Paul was from the Jewish tradition of Jerusalem while their background and faith experiences were from the Roman world. Aquila and Priscilla, not Paul, were able to teach Apollo, a new convert and new preacher, who came to Corinth. God means for us to live in relationships of learning and work. Jesus chose disciples (learners) to learn together under His teaching. When Paul discovered the value of Christian companionship he stayed in Corinth longer than anyplace so far in his journeys. It is easy to be a "Lone Ranger" in God's work today, driven by deadlines and duties. We need others, several others, to help us shape our lives, our faith and our ministries. In this environment of work and ministry, Paul was able to plant a church in the least likely place. Corinth was obviously a "Blue Collar" city and Paul learned how to minister there. The troubles of that church are well documented in Paul's letters to them. His relationship with them was obviously a two-way, open relationship that made him truly their pastor. In today's churches, we practice roles more than relationships. Pastor is on a pedestal until he fails all by himself. Other ministers suffer the same conditions only in lesser ways. The give and take of living life together is sacrificed for "the success of the church."

In Corinth, the church quickly formed itself apart from the synagogue. The Christian faith was able to move outside of the shadow of Jewish influence. The people who formed this church were directly out of paganism, as we can tell by their church behavior. Doing church in Corinth was not neat and tidy because it was a "rescue mission next door to hell." What should our churches be like? When we are so neat and tidy, who do we discourage from belonging? If we are sweet and nice all the time, do others wonder if we are "for real?" Paul found at Corinth a totally different culture than he had ever seen. He saw that the Christian faith can reach the "down and out," not just the "up and out." Paul learned the value of a long-term relationship with these people and how it was the best way to grow them in their faith. I'm sure as Paul departed Corinth, he reflected on the victories won and lives changed and the value of his ministry there. He wasn't stuck, he was settled! What are the take-a ways from this study for me? To serve God well, to be successful in what you do, to enjoy a fulfilling life, there are two lessons we can learn: *Get Your Footing Established.* If you want to throw a ball, you first get your footing set. To hit a tennis ball, golf ball, or bat in baseball, get your footing set. If you are going to have a good business, medical practice, etc., get your footing established. If you are going to serve Jesus, represent Him, speak for Him, and get your footing established.

How do you do this? We must establish a right relationship with Jesus. He is Lord! We can learn the right things by studying the scriptures and helpful books. We should trust His Holy Spirit, because He will never fail you. We can rest in the Lord, relax and let Him use you. *Get Your Message Right.* Paul struggled with his message. We have a political phrase, "getting and staying on Message." What is our message and how consistent are we in proclaiming it? We must know and experience the message that He wants us to give. We must be confident of the message that it is of God! We must trust the message, and the Holy Spirit to be supportive of the message. We must speak the message, confidently, clearly, lovingly and faithfully!

Paul, in his letter to the Romans, asked the key question. *"How can they call on him if they have not believed? And how can they believe in Him if they have not heard the message? And how can they hear of him if the message is not preached? And how can the message be preached if the messengers are not sent?"* (Romans 10: 14-15)

[FINANCES]

DEVELOPING A THEOLOGY OF CHRISTIAN
STEWARDSHIP FOR YOURSELF AND THE CHURCH

CHAPTER EIGHT:

THE BIVOCATIONAL PASTOR, FINANCE AND COMPENSATION

PHILIPPIANS 4:14

During the Watergate controversy that drove President Nixon to resignation, the quote that explains what caused it was "follow the money." Nothing profound in that statement - we do that constantly. We look for bargains; we price houses, cars and clothing; we hear that everybody has his price.

Churches are always under the microscope about how they handle their money. Those who do not appreciate the work of the church attack this subject and hypocrites in the church as their first criticisms. Most serious (and not so serious) controversies consistently have an element of money, how it is secured, used and reported. However, the church has financed itself through freewill giving since the New Testament church days.

As a bivocational pastor, you will pastor the financial life of the church. This includes how the appeal for giving is made, how the handling of all money is managed, how the money is dispersed and then reported.

This is not to say you are responsible for all of this, but you are responsible to give guidance to church leaders and members. This is very important to every element of your ministry and the ministry of the church.

You church will have developed an approach of giving and a process for receiving, spending and reporting the gift funds. As bivocational pastor, you should become acquainted with these processes as soon as possible. You will want to study financial reports from past years and past months. The church treasurer is often the best person to help you understand these. Your purpose in this study is to understand, not question or debate any part of it. If there are things that you feel need attention, save those for future discussion. It will help you understand your church's financial program by learning to know about how long the treasurer has been serving, attitude he or she has about the position and perhaps the recent history of treasurers that have served. You will also want to know how the pastor you follow handled this area of ministry.

Every church, very small to large, should have an annual budget that has been approved by vote of the church. Failure to do so tells you they have not given attention to the planning and stewardship process of the church. Consider yourself as pastor an equal member of all leadership groups, including finance committees. Quietly learn all you can, ask pertinent questions and save your thoughts for a future day if possible.

Let's start with some elementary definitions.

† Money is coined life. It is your time, energy, skills and interest traded for exchangeable coins that you can use at the stores and banks to acquire something you want.

† Gifts of money are the way the church operates its ministries. Gifts are made by members who want to support these ministries and others who make a gift from time to time.

† Budget is the spending plan of the church, the plan of how the church will support these ministries. This document should be created prayerfully by church leaders and approved by the membership through a church-wide vote.

† Stewardship is the Biblical word describing how members manage all of their money, including a portion that should be a gift to the church.

Sorry to be so elementary, but the bivocational

pastor is the shepherd of the people, how they view giving in their lives to their church and how they view the ninety percent left for personal use. Your goal will be to remind people about giving as often as you do about prayer. Most churches have used as motivation for giving, the ministries that a person's giving supports. This is a valid reason to give and this can be done by education about all the good done by ministries of the church. A second motivation for giving that need to be stressed more is what giving does in our personal life. I have found that faithful givers have learned to live by faith, find their security in God's promises and have developed happy, blessed lives as they have grown in their giving.

There was a time when many pastors felt uncomfortable preaching and leading in stewardship. Often they thought they may be accused of self-interest, raising money for their salary. That is a trap I blame on the devil. A study of the Apostle Paul's appeal for giving in 2 Corinthians 8:1 - 9:15 shows you the many motivations he gave for giving. Paul also reminds his young pastors that, just as the oxen deserves to partake from the crops, the minister is "worthy of his portion."

Part of being a pastor is to help people grow in their giving. I have discovered that the happiest people in any church are those who are generous givers. The grouchiest persons are most often the poorest givers. Here are some simple but helpful things you can do as pastor to encourage giving.

† Give a tithe yourself. Don't flaunt it, but do not hide it.

† Lead in receiving the offering. Always have a special word, scripture, illustration or encouragement prior to the prayer for the offering.

† Lead in introduction of the new annual budget to the congregation and asking for an approving vote.

† Preach about giving, not just to meet the budget needs, but also the spiritual blessings to the givers.

† Ask the congregation to respond in some way to the preaching and information on stewardship. An interesting thing to do is to set a Sunday for "Bring the Tithe" day to demonstrate what the church could do. If you do this, use the first Sunday of a month to get a true picture of the church's tithe. A more accurate and effective thing to do is to have a "Bring the Tithe" month, where a person will have a month to see the results in their life and in the church.

† Take special offerings. Many people, pastors and

church leaders, are critical of special offerings. My experience is that a limited number of special offerings, three to four, help people learn to give. Those not giving regularly will make a gift and receive a blessing and regular givers will give an added amount and find that this is both possible and pleasurable.

† Don't avoid or dictate church financial affairs. If you have a person who dominates the financial program, pray for the opportunity to talk to them. If you feel others know more than you do about the church finances, remind yourself you are a good financial supporter, your insight as a new set of eyes is very helpful and your roles as God's appointed pastor empowers you to speak up when necessary.

Here are some simple but helpful things you can do as pastor to encourage giving.

† Here are some safety steps to avoid major problems.

† Have all money counted by at least two persons and locked for deposit.

† Have all checks from the church require two signatures.

† Publish and distribute monthly financial reports, including all funds of the church.

† Insist on an annual audit, even if it is conducted by a qualified volunteer.

† Save all monthly or annual reports for seven years.

Your Compensation

When you are called to be the bivocational pastor, you will have had a serious discussion of your salary and benefits. In smaller churches there is no set formula to use in setting that amount. Here is some helpful information.

† While the accurate word is "salary," the real word is "support." There are no funds that could pay me for some of the things I have done as pastor. However, because of my family and my needs for income, the church "supports" my ministry.

† If you are coming to a church where there have been previous pastors, you have an amount to begin with. Learn about the financial circumstances surrounding that amount, the congregational conditions and how that amount has changed or remained unchanged. How does the pastor's salary amount fit into the size of the total budget? Is it 50%, 40%, 30%? What other personnel costs does the church have?

† List and evaluate your needs. These may be different than previous pastors. Without disclosing your needs list, consider how the amount in place will fit your needs. Share your concerns openly and honestly.

† Consider how the church pays the salary and how that would work for you. Are taxes deducted by the church? Is the payment period weekly, bi-weekly or monthly? Are there any benefits provided and which benefits do you need?

† Remember that the amount you negotiate may be the one you live with for a lengthy period. Is there an agreement to consider a salary adjustment each year?

As we said earlier, there is no formula to use in establishing the pastor's salary. It is true that the amount and terms need to be pleasing to both parties.

Conclusion

Jesus spoke more about money than He did about heaven and hell combined. He condemned giving to demonstrate religion and affirmed the widow who gave only two mites. He taught that *"It is more blessed to give than to receive"*(Acts 20:35), and promised *"give and it will be given to you"* (Luke 6:38). He honored the young boy who gave his lunch and led Zacheaus to give sacrificially from his wealth.

Most important, Jesus gave Himself and His life as a living sacrifice for our sins. His gift, gives us forgiveness for our sins, life that can be lived abundantly and an eternal home in Heaven. Giving is a characteristic of Jesus we must have to represent Jesus well.

RECOMMENDED RESOURCES
FOR THIS CHAPTER

Bickers, Dennis W. (2004). *The Bivocational Pastor*: Beacon Hill Press.

Hawkins, O. S. (2006). *The Pastor's Primer*: Guidestone.

SERMON RESOURCES

Church On A New Level
Matthew 16:13-20

The Bible contains two major stories:

† The Old Testament is the story of the how God created and guided persons to become a God centered nation with the mission of representing God to all nations. This nation, Israel, was blessed to become a powerful nation and then to being a slave nation to another powerful nation. Their journey to power and then to slavery is marked by the compromises of their mission by their leaders and their failure to obey God as a people.

† New Testament contains the continuing story of the New Israel: the Church. The church was designed by Jesus and was considered to be the continuing body of Christ with the mission of representing Jesus in that world and in ours. Birthed suddenly

at Pentecost, the church as described by Stephen and championed by Paul began to be established in major cities through the gentile world.

In Matthew 16, Jesus came to one of those early defining moments – defining the goal of His ministry – the church, the core issues, and the true mission of this movement. The time had come for Jesus to take His disciples, and His movement, to a new level. These disciples had followed him faithfully, hearing his teaching, watching the miracles happen, healings performed, multitudes fed from a boys lunch; They had also enjoyed being in the center of all of this, listening to the people amazed, or confused, or threatened by Jesus' ministry. They had fielded questions from the crowd, and talked among themselves about all that was happening.

Jesus knew it was time to talk with them about all of these. It was time to review these experiences, condense the talk, and crystallize their views. It was time to give definition to what this whole thing was about. It was time to take His ministry to a new level! He called this ministry "church". For the first time He used that word, named His movement, "I will build my church".

We are the church. We are the church that Jesus is talking about. Let's define who we are, what we are to do, how to do this. Churches operate on certain levels, and we are always being called to new levels of ministry. Sometimes our level is a "status quo" place, "we've never done it that way before" the standard. Sometimes our level is moving downward, making decisions, or not making them that take it lower. Sometimes we choose to move up to a new level. This takes major effort, decisive action.

Your church has committed itself to always be moving to new levels of ministry, and you have been challenged to invest in that new level.

† It will be challenging, at times bumpy, costly, to move to a new level;

† But it is much more fulfilling than living in churches "on hold" or dying;

† The Journey is never over, never arrived, always moving;

Your church can have a greater ministry, move to a new level, and join Christ in the building of His church. You may not be like a neighboring church, or like the church of your past, but you can be a growing, "moving to the next level" church. We can learn from Jesus and His disciples about that process. What are the key ingredients He needs to "build my church"? Do we have those? What can we do to move our church forward?

Jesus brought His disciples together for a defining moment. He started with exploring what they had heard and seen. "Who do men say I am?"

† Then He moved to a very personal level - "Who do you believe I am?" This is the key issue – overshadows all other issues;

† Simon, easily the spokesperson, answered for the group - "You are the Christ!"

With that statement, and the convictions behind it, Christ defined church in a clear and challenging way.

Church Is People

"You are Simon"

Look at the members of this first church - fishermen, tax collectors, zealots. Ordinary people - prone to being power hungry, hypocritical, cowardly, even betrayers, just like some of us. They became household names - Peter, Andrew, James, John, Matthew, even Judas.

He would build His church on people

Insiders like this group, Paul said of one church, "And such were some of you." "We do not all sin alike, but we are alike in that we sin." All Sinners! Outsiders who will need to be included (they have not arrived yet); spiritually hungry, but not "church" hungry; five generations in one society, all different looking for different words, music, values;

But Changing People

"You are Simon - You will be Peter." Not quickly, not easily, Simon would spend the rest of his life becoming the Rock. From a loud, boisterous, violent, betraying, guilty person, who religious leaders would call a "zero", not important. See his struggle to change in Acts!

We Must Always Be a Changing Person

Q. How many church members does it take to change a light bulb?

A. Who said anything about change?

We Change Or We Die

† Our bodies change, totally renewing itself every seven years;

† Our society is in the midst of one of the most dramatic change periods in history;

† Churches must change, books tell us;

† "Meltdown In The Mainline"

† "Dying For Change"

Old systems are designed only to maintain the status quo, and can't take us to a new level of ministry. Systems can carry the message!

Church Has A Central Principle

An organizing principle, a principle held in common by the people of church - "Thou Art The Christ". This was the central truth that gave meaning to all Jesus did. There could have been several answers:

† Great teacher, great prophet, great leader; conservative, liberal, smart, rebellious -

† "You Are The Christ" - One sent from God; anointed of God; Son of God;

† This was to be the central truth that emerged out of the suffering, sorrow, shame of the next few months

† Only the Christ could suffer, die, and be raised from the dead!

This is the central message, the organizing principle of true church today. "Jesus Talk" is everywhere, even when church is seen as negative.

† We are different as persons, but we have a common conviction - Jesus is the Christ, God's sent one to us.

† An "8 Track Church in a CD World", Robert Nash admonishes us to stick with the central story - the story of Jesus. *"If I be lifted up, I will draw all men unto me."*

† In a film produced for BBC about homeless people, they recorded a street man who constantly sang "Jesus never failed me yet".

Church Has An Eternally Significant Purpose!

This is awesome:

† "Who you bind on earth will be bound in heaven, and who you loose on earth will be loosed in heaven!"

† You have a mission and purpose to set people free; sponsor personal resurrections, set free those in slavery.

Church is for Everyone

† Those inside this congregation, who are bound by rules & rituals, who struggle to make life work seven days a week, who believe in Christ but have not claimed His power; who hunger for others to journey with in faith;

† Those outside, the church exists for those who never come near it.

Church Has Commanding Power; Driving Power"

"the gates of hell will not defeat you"

There was a time when church was a dominant force in society - a popular place to go, a right thing to do, and laws protected its turf. But it is not so now. We have become marginal in our influence, minimal in our influence. In a popular stereotype found in *Bury My Heart At Wounded Knee*, the chief refused to have a church built because "all they do is divide and fight"

Power, but not Automatic power

Henri Nouwen went from a professorship at Harvard to be priest at Daybreak, a community for intellectually handicapped persons. In that setting nothing he had been or done, tithes, books, resumes, mattered to his parishioners. Only one thing was important, their question was "Do you love me?"

Jesus forced Peter, after all of the crucifixionand resurrection events, to answer one question - "Do you love me?" The church that loves Jesus and loves people will move to a new level.

[PERSONAL LIFE]

AVOID BURNOUT THROUGH TIME WITH
FAMILY, FRIENDS AND GOD

CHAPTER NINE:

THE BIVOCATIONAL PASTOR AND PERSONAL LIFE ISSUES

"*11* Only Luke is with me. Get Mark and bring him
with you, for he is useful to me for ministry. *12*
And Tychicus I have sent to Ephesus. *13* Bring the
cloak that I left with Carpus at Troas when you
come—and the books, especially the parchments."

2 TIMOTHY 4:11-13

Every area of ministry has unique benefits, and this is
true of the bivocational pastor. The important thing is
to find the ministry place and its' benefits that fit you.

The bivocational pastor's role, one person in two
distinct career or job roles, can be a blessing. I have
served both as a full-time pastor and in two work areas
parallel to each other. My first career path was as a full-
time pastor for about 25 years. Although I enjoyed that
ministry, I found myself bored quite often. I also found
that I could not do much to increase my income level

regardless of my effectiveness. In a midlife change, I moved into the church fund-raising profession, raising funds for church buildings. In the next 25 years, I helped raise millions of dollars through church building campaigns, serving more than 200 churches. I also was able to increase my income to levels I had never thought possible. In those first two chapters of life, I felt both God's guidance and blessing. In this present part of life, which I call my "third-half," both of those ministry areas, preaching and fund-raising, are both blessed in my life.

There are benefits. As a full-time pastor, 90% of my regular contacts were within the church. Now a large portion of my contacts are outside of the local congregation. As a full-time pastor, my one source of income was the church. Sometimes this can create anxiety. As a bivocational pastor I have two sources of income, providing me a sense of security and independence. As a pastor, I often sensed that I and my family lived in a glass house. That is not true of my bivocational ministry. Finally, as a full-time pastor, I felt the expectations of the people were unrealistic. Now the church people have very limited expectations and it is enjoyable to exceed those expectations.

As an essential part of the bivocational role is to be in or find a work apart from the church that is flexible enough to match the bivocational ministry schedule and demands. In this book, I can imagine a bivocational schedule as simple as Sunday activities with some unexpected demands to a bivocational role that may require more of a person's time on some occasions and a second work taking up a majority of workdays. The most important thing to remember is the importance of doing all your work well as a witness of your Christian life.

Whatever the demands of each role, the bivocational pastor must learn the skill of time and work management. There are several sources to help in this area. Many are as complicated as double entry bookkeeping and other as simple as working off a calendar or a daily to-do list. I have a suggestion on how to build your time and work management plan. You can put your life's details in the plan, regardless of how many or few hours you have to invest in the ministry area of your life. Here is a starter list.

† You have *committed time,* like time for the scheduled activities of the church.

† *Family time* must be reserved or it will disappear.

† *Study time* is an essential part of a quality ministry. Preaching time comes quickly, week after week.

† *People time* with the people in your congregation

is necessary to maintain good relationships and to flavor your preaching with people's needs.

† *God time* - your time with God not for preaching, by praying, not for bragging purposes, but building your daily relationship with God.

You will know what hours you have available and how much time you can devote to each area. However, you structure this plan. The key to success is self-discipline. Let me give you an example of my failure to discipline my study life. This illustration would fit well in the chapter on being the pastor.

As pastor of a First Baptist Church near the Baptist seminary in Kentucky, I enjoyed relating to the seminary and having some faculty visit our church often. One specific faculty member, a preaching professor, would visit often when they visited their family nearby. It had been one of those weeks where I conducted three funerals, attended two denominational meetings and postponed sermon preparation to the end of the week. I came to the pulpit that Sunday with what I called a "Saturday night special," a poor excuse for a sermon. That morning as I visited among the pews, I noticed that the preaching professor was back with his wife. When I greeted him, he introduced me to his guest. It was the complete preaching faculty of Southern Baptist Theological Seminary and their wives. The phrase, "want to get away" fit the occasion so well. I'm sure my sermon was an example in their teaching the next week on how to preach badly. Looking back with embarrassment, I learned how important the discipline of sermon preparation time is.

The center of your personal life is your family. While other challenges such as the church can be put aside for a period of time, your family life is forever the biggest source of pleasure and responsibility. While other families in the church have a pastor to walk with them in times of stress, your family has you as husband, father and pastor.

The pastor's wife can be the pastor's best friend and advocate. Many times the pastor's wife has struggled to be that to a husband who is preparing to be a pastor. The early years of the marriage can be tough and the pastor's wife can be wounded before the real ministry journey begins. The early years of ministry in which the two amateurs try to learn the correct way to fulfill their roles can be difficult. When a pastor loses his wife and family through divorce, he loses his ministry. Don't let that happen to you!

The Bible's instructions to husbands apply to the pastor also. Those words of guidance often start with the phrase, "Husbands, love. . ." The ultimate statement is *"Love your wives just as Christ loved the church and gave himself for her"* (Ephesians 5:25). Dr. O S. Hawkins, in his book *The Pastor's Primer,* underscores the role of the pastor-husband as being both "provider" and "protector" for his wife and family.

That same role of provider-protector applies to the pastor's children with one addition, "parent." Being a parent is one of the most joyful experiences of a lifetime. The ingredients of parenting include unlimited love, grace, forgiveness and some tangible things as blocks of time, good example, words of guidance and expressions of pride and appreciation for each child. While these are lofty words and our loyalty and love are consistent, the journey is often rocky.

A pastor friend named Larry was a very effective pastor at the peak of his ministry. He and his wife were excellent parents. However, his life was turned upside down when his son was arrested for using and selling drugs. He now faced the challenge of helping his son restructure his life, plus the embarrassment of the community knowing this news. He called the deacons of the church together, explained his troubles, read his resignation letter and put it on the conference room table. No one picked up the letter or spoke for a few minutes. Then the chairman spoke and said, "Welcome to the real world, pastor. Most of us in this room have also experienced this in some form with our children. We will not accept your resignation. You are still our pastor and we all need you. We will pray for you and help you when we can."

As a pastor, personal care of yourself is also essential to your ministry. This includes your personal health and well-being. No one else is more responsible for your physical and emotional health than you. I have seen many pastors serve with no regard for their health, become overweight or emotionally fatigued and have health problems before they get a good start. Good exercise and eating habits can lengthen the life of your ministry. Lengthening your life is good stewardship of your usefulness to God.

This is also true of your personal finances. In our world of costly purchases and high debt load, the danger of financial disaster is not far away. Your personal finances are always a two person responsibility and it is essential that both persons are consistently engaged. While one of the two may feel that they are most qualified to be the hands-on manager, there must be common consent of who that should be. The two must also agree on their financial priorities, the bills to be paid each month and any new expenditures. A financial bankruptcy will follow you for many years, and cripple your personal life and your ministry.

One investment you can make in your future is to continue your education. Education for the proper purposes is still an investment that cannot be taken from you. You will be wise to develop for yourself a plan of continuing education. There are many ways to develop your skills through seminars, workshops and on-line learning opportunities. Skill development in the key areas of preaching, church growth, counseling, social skills and understanding people will strengthen your ministry immediately. There are many ways to continue your formal education in theory. Biblical studies and ministry understanding while at the same time earn some credentials to enhance your value to churches.

There are countless schools and organizations that offer these classes on line. My wife and I have served for several years with Newburg Bible College and Seminary in Indiana. The president, Dr. Glenn Mollette, seeks to provide quality ministry education for a moderate cost to fit the diverse needs of today's God-called ministers. The online format for this training allows anyone, with any personal schedule, from any spot on the globe, to earn credentials and gain knowledge for ministry.

One area of personal care of ourselves I want to cautiously address is your personal appearance. The styles of dress for ministers have thankfully changed. The stereotype of suit and tie for all occasions is gone. It is interesting that ministers of a specific area of church work still dress alike. Have you been to a meeting of church planters, where almost everyone is wearing jeans and a colored plaid shirt worn not tucked in? Most established churches are led by ministers who love golf shirts, regardless of how tight they fit. They have become like the teenagers who want to be different so they all dress alike.

I believe that it is still true that the person dressed attractively gets waited on first. They are also noticed most often and remembered the longest. I know that being all dressed up often evokes the question, "Are you a preacher?" When a pastor dresses for the day, he dresses for office time, hospital visits, prospective luncheon and possibly the funeral home. A sharp shirt and khaki slacks makes a good appearance in all of those places. Shined shoes help the image. We only have one time to make a first impression.

A Final Thought

Let's talk about BURNOUT. Every career path is experiencing burnout among their brightest and best. I remember the time I was the pastor of a significant church where I experienced burnout. I would often drive by the church, look at the tallest steeple in the country, read the church sign with the wrought iron letters spelling my name, and wonder why I was not happy. My story has been repeated in the lives of other pastors thousands of times. May I help you avoid burnout?

Burnout is emotional fatigue. Often we experience emotional fatigue when we retreat from relationships with others. Our reasons for retreat can be countless. We each create our own. We experience this when, retreating from others, we try to live like a "Long Ranger." We experience emotional fatigue and retreat into isolation, when the relationships of our life are out of line. It can be with our spouse, our church leaders or the family. We experience emotional fatigue when we retreat into loneliness and try to function from there, totally disconnected from significant people in our lives.

Burnout is often caused by the lack of self esteem. As a pastor of a small rural church, you may begin to feel second class as a pastor. Everyone else is better off than you. You may feel your educational background is not good enough, your record of attendance and baptisms are disgraceful and you aren't paid very much. Your self esteem tank is empty, but you dare not tell anyone about it.

I want to explore with your some possible areas of future trouble that you can deal with before your crash landing.

† The *"Failure Cycle:"* Failure is a part of attempting

things beyond our usual level of work. Ministry is always an exercise of possible success and failure. Like a baseball batter who gets in a batting slump, we have ministry slumps also. Some of the failures we reflect on are related to big projects or very important change possibilities. After we invest in these, we have absolutely no control over the decision to implement.

† The *"People Pleasing"* Syndrome: Most of us have an appreciation for people's thankfulness for our presence and help. "People pleasing" is when we become addicted to the rewards of the behavior and can't get enough.

† The *Values Clash:* Ministry is all about very important values. Sometimes we fail to implement some of them in our lives. We then judge ourselves to be moral or spiritual failures.

† The *Family Crisis:* Even when we understand the importance of family values, we choose to travel another way. Whether it is a wayward child or a third-party relationship, these crises rob our lives of the power and personal pride to be a preacher and leader.

† The *Isolation Trap:* Whatever the real problem is,

the resulting behavior is often to isolate ourselves from others, try to continue our ministry as a wounded warrior and cut well-meaning people out of our lives.

You may be able to bring other causes to this discussion. You can create your own scenarios and even feel worse. What can you do to avoid or overcome burnout? Here's a short list:

† Do a truthful, stern evaluation of your emotional and spiritual life. What is there in *your life that is running your battery down?* Often we have *inappropriate relationships* or habits that are like battery cables, hitting together to empty our emotional battery instantly. What is there in your *daily routine that is* sapping you of energy? This may be a *conflict* with church leaders or an *avoidance of specific duties* that you are not doing. Scott Peck says that "avoidance is the beginning of mental illness." I have found this to be true. If I've missed your battery sapper, please write it in now.

† Grow your self-esteem. When your self-esteem tank is empty, it has been bombarded by several negative messages sent constantly to put you down. However, most of these messages are composed and sent by you. You can do better than that. Sit

down each day and compose a new set of positive messages. Do not allow any negative messages to be sent. In your prayer life, confess to God briefly your problem and ask for His help. Do this every day for the rest of your life.

† Start a new daily schedule with your new positive messages. Get out of the house early, go drink coffee at the nearest Hardees, plan some visits and be sure you make them. Set up a study schedule for your sermons. Plan a new series of sermons, perhaps on David's moments of victory. The book on David by Max Lucado is a very good source. Read for twenty minutes from a positive thinking book. Maintain a daily habit of personal Bible reading.

† Keep a record each day of your victories; dismiss the memory of your failures. Perhaps sit down each evening and on a special pad, (like a stenographer's spiral pad), list your victories and give thanks the next day in your prayer time.

† You might consider visiting your doctor for his analysis of your health and advice on medications.

† Do some form of brisk outdoor exercise each day. Develop a routine that is comfortable for you that takes about 40 minutes to do. If you do not have an

attractive place to go out near your home, go to a park or greenway trail.

† Get close to God, both in your devotional time and throughout the day. Have a time of prayer with as many individuals as you can each day. Live in His presence as much as you can.

May I add one unattractive possibility in our personal life-experiencing burnout? In a book written to persons new to the bivocational ministry or considering it, this may feel like an inappropriate negative message. I am convinced that many who suffer burnout have the seeds of the experience in their early years and can correct them.

Simply stated, burnout is a state of physical, mental, spiritual and emotional exhaustion caused by extended and intense levels of stress. It leads to the questioning of one's ability and/or the value of one's worth. This often takes years of service and several changes in locations to accumulate enough negative experience to lead to a vocational breakdown. Here is another "to-do" list that I practice.

† Make your marriage and your family your top priority. Marriages fail even in the pastor's home. Children are prone to make questionable decisions, but they are less likely to do so when they know how

much their parents love and trust them.

† Learn to know and understand yourself. Have a sense of your level of self-esteem and your confidence in your ability to face tough times.

† Value your faith in God as more than being good in your ministry career. Your life of faith is a life lived in the presence of God. God is a God of grace and personal relationships.

† Know that God forgives us much more easily than we forgive ourselves. Put your failures in your rear-view mirror and keep moving forward.

† Your Christian friends and supporters in the church are kind and loving. They want you to grow, progress in ministry and live a good life.

Mark the parts of this chapter that were helpful to you and return each week to review them. Share this chapter with other pastor friends.

RECOMMENDED RESOURCES
FOR THIS CHAPTER

Bennis, Warren & Nanus, Bart (2003). *Leaders: Strategies For Taking Charge:* Alban Institute.

Bickers, Dennis W. (2004). *The Bivocational Pastor:* Beacon Hill Press.

Hawkins, O. S. (2006). *The Pastor's Primer:* Guidestone.

<u>SERMON RESOURCES</u>

Overcoming the Stuck Places
Acts 20:22-27; Acts 21:27-33

We all encounter "stopping places", places where the obstacles are so huge that they stop our forward progress in life. Often these become "stuck places", places where we never get moving again. In today's scripture, the apostle Paul came to a possible major "stopping place", possibly a "stuck" place that tested his resolve for his God-given mission and a place where his ministry was radically changed. To put Paul's experiences in contemporary contexts, here are three very likely examples happening today. A bright young man from an extremely dysfunctional family married a beautiful lady and, as a bonus, he was included in a wonderful, loving family that taught him so much about marriage and family. He and his wife visited his family often with very brief visits but the occasion came that they must make an extended visit. During those days they endured arguments and word fights that were hard for them to sit through. On one of those occasions, the young man tried to settle the quarrel. A fight broke out, the police were called in and he was arrested as the trouble maker.

A student went away from home for his first year of college. He had been raised to faithfully attend and participate in a very formal, ritualistic, liturgical church. When he arrived at college, he began to attend a spirited, joyful Christian gathering very different from his church experience. He discovered he could have a personal experience and relationship with Jesus and he enjoyed the free, charismatic worship services they held. He came home for a vacation time and returned to his home church. He began to talk with members and leaders about what he had experienced, how things were done in his group and asking why that could not happen there. Soon the church officials tired of his talk and questions and asked him not to come back. A bank officer of an older, traditional bank was being groomed to be the next president and was sent to a banker's training course in a major city. There he learned how other, more progressive banks were doing things that made sense and were good business practices. When he returned home he began to talk up these changes, implement those he could and debate with his fellow junior officers why these things could not work. Soon his peer officers, not wanting change, accused him of embezzlement, had him arrested and fired. Paul's story, wrapped around these scriptures, was remarkably similar. He was raised a loyal Jew, educated by the very best teachers, entered the ranks of the Pharisees at a young adult age and began to prove his leadership abilities by persecuting Christians. God had other plans for him! God had met Paul on the Damascus Road, dramatically saved him and called him to the pioneer task of becoming a missionary to the Gentiles. At this time in the story in Acts, Paul had conducted two missionary journeys to Gentile lands and gathered a strong supporting group of both Jews and Gentiles. In his heart he felt the need to return to Jerusalem, the center of his past life and of Jewish religious heritage, and plead with them to consider accepting Jesus as their Messiah. His friends tried to stop him, knowing the danger he faced. Ray Steadman, a respected New Testament scholar, has declared that Paul made a major mistake in doing this.

Paul visited with James, the leader of the Jewish Christians in Jerusalem. A plan was accepted that Paul

would go to the temple, the Jewish holy place, participate in a renewal dedication ceremony called a "Naza-
rite Vow" and sponsor four others who wanted to do
the same. This was Paul's way of being acceptable to his
old friends and peers in the Jewish hierarchy. He was
quickly recognized by the leaders of the group that con-
tested his teachings in the synagogues in the Gentile
territories. The leader and others organized a massive
revolt to his presence in the temple. The Roman guards
were called in to restore peace and Paul was arrested.
Paul's ministry was radically changed. He spent the
rest of his life going from jail to jail, defending himself and his faith before governors and kings, writing
to people he had hoped to physically visit and later
marched to his death an older, weakened man. Paul
spoke of being "bound by the Spirit" to go to Jerusalem. He left the city bound by Roman chains. The contrast he offers is the difference between "religion" and
living with Jesus. The word religion comes from the
Latin word "religie", which means "to bind." Everyone
is bound by their convictions, culture and interpreta-
tion of life. The Book of Acts describes a life of spirit-
led freedom and the last verse of the book speaks of
the gospel preached "unhindered," that is "not bound"!
What are the characteristics of the Apostle Paul that
gave him the freedom from being "stopped" and "stuck"

in these circumstances? What are the resources he had that we can develop in our lives as Christ's followers? First, I suggest that Paul had a "Decided Heart." This phrase comes from the book, "*The Traveler's Gift*," by Andy Andrews. In his seven characteristics of a successful life, this is the central one, number four of seven. The "Decided Heart" is not concerned with "I might, I ought or I can't." Perhaps the youth chorus, "I have decided to follow Jesus" says it best, "No turning back." In his novel, "*The Mended Heart*," Andy Andrews describes two people thrown together by chance. The girl was a recent widow of World War II who came to the gulf coast to care for her dying aunt and to nurse her own broken heart. The man was a German soldier from a submarine that invaded the Gulf of Mexico to sink ships carrying supplies to soldiers in Europe. He had been wounded, swam ashore by night and lay dying on the beach. She discovered him and hated him because his people had killed her young husband. The story brings the two together to marry. In his research of the story, Andy Andrews had consulted an older couple in his church for facts on the case. Later he discovered that this older couple was the two characters in this story. Their hearts mended by their love of each other and the "Decided Heart" is developed by the hard circumstances of life and their decision to forgive that either make or break any of us. A second resource that enables Paul to be the victor over these obstacles is his God-given mission. When he met God on the Damascus Road, God told Paul he was to be "missionary to the Gentiles, kings and all Israel." Such a calling is a powerful force in life. It is a fact that all of us have a calling, a mission for life. The business principle may fit here, "begin with the end in mind." We may not know, as Paul did not know, exactly how the end will be but when we begin with His mission as ours, the end will be good. The Taylor family, living in England in the early 1800's, had two sons. The older son became a lawyer, a member of parliament and gained prestige. The second son, Hudson, felt his mission in life was to be a missionary to China. He made a covenant with God, sailed to China and went into the inland where missionaries had never been. He learned the language, dressed like the people, ate their food and lived among them. His most prominent characteristic was "unreserved commitment." The first son's name is never mentioned. He is always described as "a brother to Hudson Taylor." There is power in our mission for life. A third characteristic of Paul and others who have a "decided heart" and do life with their mission in mind, is that they accept life as God directs them. A life directed by God has movement and meaning. It may not be the plans we want, the circumstances or the results that we would chose, but it is a life lived for God. Perhaps 500 years ago the Durer family lived in Nuremburg, Germany. There were 18 children in the family. The father was a goldsmith and did other chores to provide for his family but there was no way for the children to advance beyond the wage-earner life. Two of the boys, Albert and Albrecht, vowed to move ahead. They agreed that one of them would go on to higher education supported by the other and then they would reverse order. They flipped a coin to decide who would go first and Albrecht won the toss. He went to an arts academy while Albert worked in the mines to support him. Albrecht learned well, became a noted artist and earned large fees for his work. He returned to his village and family in celebration of his success. When Albrecht rose to speak, he told about the agreement with his brother and said, "Albert, now it's your turn." Albert began to say no and finally stood to speak. "I cannot go for training. In the last four years my hands have been so damaged. My fingers have been mashed and I cannot hold a brush to do the fine lines necessary for art. It is too late for me." You may not be familiar of the art work of Albrecht Durer's other art work, but you know of one. Albrecht drew his brother's hands, scared, twisted fingers, palms together and fingers painted upward in prayer. We know of it as "Praying Hands", a memorial to the life of his brother. God takes our circumstances, our resources and directs them in such a way that they are His masterpiece, not ours.

The fourth characteristic of Paul's life and ministry was his championing of God's grace, not law. His visit to the capital of legalism, Jerusalem, is reflected in all of his writing, especially the Book of Romans. Martin Luther discovered this truth in Paul's word, "for by grace are you saved." The church Paul planted in Corinth is a demonstration of what grace can do. The people we meet in those two books are former pagans, today's converts and tomorrow's saints. They found it hard to overcome their behavior of paganism, their selfishness, human pride and their old ways of thinking. Paul coached them, criticized them and prayed them into being a workable "body of Christ." He reminds these and others by listing a number of the worst sins of the flesh and saying, "and such were some of you." Our final characteristic of Paul's life that comes from his Jerusalem experience was this: He knew the end of his story, and it was good. He truly "began with the end in mind" and rejoiced in that moment. Often, in the midst of his hard life, he would wonder if it might be better to go be with God than to be in his circumstances. However, when the moments came that his death was near, his body tired, his execution scheduled, he could write, "I have fought a good fight, I have finished the course… and there is laid up for me a crown of righteousness." Are you stuck? Find yourself in a stopping place? Wondering what God wants from you? Here is a simple four line poem that may help you.

You ask, what is the will of God?

Well, here is the answer true.

The nearest thing that should be done,

That He can do-through you.

[BALANCED LIFE]

EXERCISING PRIORITIES, PLANNING, PRACTICE AND DISCIPLINE

CHAPTER TEN:

THE BIVOCATIONAL PASTOR AND THE BALANCED LIFE

"I have fought the good fight, I have finished the race, I have kept the faith."

2 TIMOTHY 4:7

The Apostle Paul would begin this chapter with, *"and finally, brethren."* What each of us would say in this final chapter is based on where we find ourselves as we finish this conversation. I'm not at the place Paul found himself, in prison and awaiting a certain execution.

Here is my conclusion to the conversation we have had for several hours. I'm calling this chapter "Balancing the Life of a Bivocational Pastor." You may see that as impossibility, but let's give it a try. *I have Ten Top principles for you* to consider, rewrite, make them yours and live by them.

† *With God's leadership, establish priorities for your life and live by them.*

You've heard the fire drill test, "if your house was on fire and you had the opportunity to take out five things, what would they be?" Here's my Heaven's Gates test. If you suddenly arrived at Heaven's Gates and had to announce the real priorities of your life, what would they be? Remember, you've lived as long as possible and you can only establish your list by the life you can look back on, what would you say? That day will come, sooner or later. You have the opportunity to establish and live out your real priorities. Build your list and live by it.

† *Put God First! Proverbs 3:5-6 is right." Trust in the Lord with all your heart and lean not upon your own understanding. In all your ways acknowledge Him and He will direct your path."*

When your top priority is to serve and honor God, you will be able to have what Jesus promised, "abundant life," and you will be able to look back upon your life today and thank Him for His abundant blessings.

† *Put your family, and your personal well-being, as your second priority and as your service to God.*

Your ministry is enhanced or diminished by your family. Your marriage is very important to the quality of your life and the witness of your faith. The love you share with your family is an example of the grace and love you share in your ministry.

    † *Know your purpose in life and embrace this as your mission for God.*

The Apostle stated, "This one thing I do." Your ministry can be distorted by a lack of purpose. While many purposes are worthy of your attention, a laser-like focus on the purpose God has for you will be your key to eternal success.

    † *Manage your time, energy and emotions as your daily service for God.*

Your daily time, energy and emotional strength are like a daily investment in a great cause. Great fortunes and organizations are not built by a few large investments or surges, but by the regular, faithful investments of caring persons. Your daily time, energy and emotions are gifts from God and you will choose how you spend them

    † *Learn to be proactive, instead of reactive.*

Life presents each of us opportunities and obstacles. One reaction to these will shape our lives and legacies. The choices involved in these are very important. As a minister, those around you will have diverse expectations. We are people of faith, but not foolish. Such is the tensions of the right response. We will need to know all the facts, look carefully at the options and prayerfully seek God's guidance. When possible, we should be on the side of faith, love and vision.

Live with a clear conscience, both before God and others.

Our self-esteem is really our consciousness of our value. This is like a bank account with the balance established by our deposits and withdrawals. The withdrawals are occasions when we spend some of our value to satisfy a need of ourselves or others. Our deposits are those times when we make good choices, meet the needs of others and sense the approval of God. Although all of these factors can be manipulated, the bottom line is "we make our choices, and our choices make us."

† *Enjoy friendships with many persons and invest often in them.*

While we speak often in this chapter about investing, one of the best areas of investment of time and interest is with friends. I've met some people who over-invested in others, and made poor choices of who they invested in. I've also met persons who invested in careers, possessions and other personal choices and finished life an unhappy person. The choice is always in moderation, and good friends are hard to find, especially in hard times.

† *Give careful attention to your emotional well-being.*

Ministry is an exercise in controlled emotions. You will find yourself making hospital calls, moving from one floor where you rejoice with the parents of a new child and going to another floor to weep with those whose loved one is dying. We stand and joyfully preach a sermon on salvation and then sit down in the office to try to help a person who has wrecked his life with one bad decision. Sit down often; invite God to join you as you try to return to the place of emotional peace.

† *Realize you are not superman. Carefully plan not to burn out, but finish well.*

The Bible often refers to life as a journey, a path that includes mountains, valleys and forest. I often stop at some quiet place and read Psalm 23. We all have witnessed our fellow pastor who suffered burn-out, leaving behind a defeated person. Seldom do we think of "finishing well" in our younger years. That is the blessing of aging. For most of us there is a chapter of life before we gain heaven. It too can be a rewarding part of life.

Your Balanced Career

The need for bivocational pastors will continue to grow in the next decades. The biggest reason is the economy. More and more churches are struggling to stay afloat financially. Everything costs more and offerings are decreasing. More churches, whose large buildings indicate larger congregations in the past, are unable to handle the maintenance cost of the building. These are skyscrapers in New York and dominate church buildings on courthouse squares. Churches are cutting back staff costs and replacing the full-time professional staff members with bivocational persons.

This also says that the quality of the bivocational minister must improve. *The bivocational pastors of tomorrow* will be better educated and skillful. Many pastors with a seminary degree will see the bivocational career choice as more attractive. Some of these will have training in a second career that they also enjoy. Many will have a small business they enjoy operating or a position in an organization that provides them another set of pleasures and benefits. Even today, there are several well known preachers who serve as preaching pastor of a large church and as teaching professor of a nearby university or college.

The role of bivocational pastor will become an attractive option for more ministers for a variety of reasons. Pastors nearing retirement age will view this option an ideal "second career." For persons like me who have never considered retirement an attractive option, and who have had a ministry career of positive experiences, it offers many fulfilling benefits. Don't be surprised to see many ministry preparatory organizations offering a credential training program for bivocational pastors.

The life expectancy of retiring pastors is rapidly expanding. Pastors are in better health and sharper mentally than their peers of twenty years ago. I remember a piece of advice I received years ago from a financial planner. "When a person reaches 65 years of age, they need to have 20 more years of life *planned*." The bivocational pastor role is a great plan. The retiring pastor can negotiate with a church a flexible schedule and available shared responsibilities to favor the retired pastor. The retired pastor can bring to the church quality, progressive leadership that can give to the church a new future.

Often when a person receives a call to ministry in his mid-life years, his first thoughts are to quit his job, move to an educational institution and start a whole new life. That may be his best option. However, if his present career path will allow it, the best option may be to continue his present work with some flexibility, enroll in a training institution with an on-line program, such as Newburg Bible College and Seminary, and find a ministry role to fill in the local area. At the end of a five to ten year period he may find he has progressed the most in his present setting. Anyone who is a bivocational pastor should never see that initial training as all there is. More opportunities to learn and grow will always be available as time moves on.

The possibilities of the bivocational pastor's career are boundless. Today's bivocational pastor should live with a vision of the future, not just for the church he services, but also for himself. The bivocational pastor's career gives a minister a wonderful opportunity of an extended ministry and longevity. It also offers spiritual and financial freedoms that will give a more expanded personal life.

The greatest challenge and opportunity for bivocational pastors today is to help the small churches that dot the landscape grow. There are those who will not survive long-term regardless of the pastor. That pastor's role is to minister to the members who are there now. There are churches that may live, but not flourish. Many of these are family-dominated churches where the challenge is to develop new leaders from both younger family members and new people who are "adopted." Some of the smaller churches are more likely to live because of leadership, location and a vision that they have a future. All smaller churches are a "niche" ministry, that is to say they will appeal to a small fraction of the population who prefer a small church. That group does exist and can be reached.

The biggest challenge of the smaller churches is

financial. Along with the fact that everything costs more, securing the best bivocational pastors and providing the best ministry programs also costs more. The churches are tested in this way. If they have progressive lay leadership who see that providing the best is essential, they will thrive as a church. If the lay leadership is cautious and there is no vision for the future, the future of the church is limited. The bivocational pastor of a small church must be able to lead the church in stewardship expansion. That emphasis must be as regular and consistent as worship and Bible study.

Bivocational pastors follow the path of New Testament heroes and later Christian leaders. Join the parade with me. You will love it!

RECOMMENDED RESOURCES
FOR THIS CHAPTER

Dale, Robert D. (2004). *Keeping The Dream Alive:* Broadman Press.

Dale, Robert D. (1998). *Leadership For A Changing Church:* Abingdon Press.

Smith, Fred & Goetz, David L. (1999). *Leading With Integrity:* Bethany House Publishers.

Sweet, Leonard (1995). *Faithquakes:* Abingdon Press.

SERMON RESOURCES

Moving Forward

JOSHUA 3:1-13

The movie, *"Prince of Egypt,"* told the story of Moses leading his people out of Egypt, but stopped before their journey in the wilderness. The real story is of their journey across the wilderness, they refused to go immediately into the Promised Land and of their 40 year wandering period in the wilderness.

Sarah Breathnach, in her daily devotional book, *"Something More",* states that there is always a wilderness on the way to our promised land. She also notes that the wilderness is not a place of punishment, of barren life and suffering. It is often a place of learning. Christ went to a wilderness to be tempted and to shape himself for His ministry; Paul spent three years at a wilderness location to prepare himself for his ministry. In Joshua 3:1-13, tells about their renewed mission – to leave their wilderness homes and to embrace the mission of their nation, to enter and live in their promised land.

They had discovered a very important principle of their mission

"They must fight for their promised land. It was already occupied with giants and experienced warriors. It was not to be a stroll into the land, but a battle for their lives and their identity."

Our church is standing at a new, challenging place in its history. For some, the past few years have been wilderness wanderings. For all of us, this is a moment of challenge. We will shape our church for its future, either intentionally by our response or unintentionally by our lack of response.

Israel had a unique DNA – no other nation was like it. Its DNA was its mission (represent God), its values (the things that matter most), their beliefs (core convictions) and their vision of the future for them.

Our church has its own DNA, unlike any other church. We cannot be a Crystal Cathedral or a Willowcreek. We must define who we are, and move forward with our uniqueness.

We Have a Mission – to lead people to know Jesus as Saviour and Lord; to grow ourselves and other to be like Jesus, whom we follow, and to go for Jesus into the world to share the good news and meet needs;

We Have Values – principles we would stand for in any battle; the value of People, all people, hurting people, little people, prominent people;

† The Bible, that speaks to real life;

† Prayer, a priority in us personally and our congregation;

† Grace, that we offer and receive grace;

† The leadership of the Holy Spirit;

We gather, as did the people of Israel, know God has blessed us in times past, and face our future – moving out of a wilderness and to the place God directs.

How do we do this? Where do we start? Let's take some clues from Joshua Chapter

† *Consecrate yourself* – the Spiritual Preparation –

† Doing Soul Work – along, personal, individually;

† This time has been labeled the 4th Great Awakening for America for American. It is a time of spiritual hunger, Chuck Colson and the Pope agree, "The year 2000 will be a springtime for Christianity;

† We talk freely of Jesus, read Spiritual books, listen to the Virgin Mary, and study about Angels;

† *Joshua called his people to <u>prepare Spiritually</u>* –

† Not practice warfare, marching, or holding a strategy session, motivational talk;

† He knew the nation would be no better than its individual members, and their relationship with God.

† Churches, our church, reflects the strengths found in us, the members.

† Being a Christian is always first an "Inside Job",

† Living with Jesus inside our being.

† There is in each of us a "Holy of Holies", a private closet. Jesus said, "The kingdom of God is within you".

† There comes a time, a holy moment, when we must meet God for a summit meeting – will it be our way, or God's way?

† Jacob was to face his angry brother and possibly be killed, but first he must wrestle with God the night before;

† Jesus faced His death on the cross, but first He must meet God in the garden;

† Paul had a passion for World Missions, but he must spend time apart to receive a call to Macedonia;

There is a story of a ruling prince who had a mis-shaped body, a crooked back. While he ruled his people well, he was never seen in public because of his deformity. One day he called a famous sculptor in, asking him to create a statue of himself, what he would look like if he didn't have the crooked back.

The statue was placed in a private corner of the garden. Often the prince would leave his office and go to that corner, to gaze at the statue. Soon those around him noticed that he was standing taller, the crook in his back less pronounced. Eventually the prince went out in public, and you could hardly see any crook in his back.

Our challenge is that as we "Look unto Jesus", our lives are shaped to be like Him.

† *"Get Up From Your Place, and March"* – Develop Fellowship, Community, *Do Relationship Work!*

† They were not just to sit alone in prayer; they were to join the march of the fellow Israelites.

† We have honored individualism as a nation, and as Baptist. Churches have been formed around lead-

ers – well-known pastors.

† The best work is always done by a team, a group;

It is harder to march with the band than march alone; harder to sing in a quartet than solo. Healing comes to the addicted person from a group, like Alcohol Anonymous.

Adam Smith, in His classic "Wealth of Nations" says that 10 people, working alone, can make 20 pins each per day; 10 people, working together, can make 48,000 pins per day.

† Difficult to build fellowship, community at church.

† We are so different, yet have one common commitment; like to work alone, do individual jobs, sing solos, (Quote:"If you are one of the herd of sheep, remember that sheep smell".)

† In Acts, the great moving experiences happened among Christians being together;

† Pentecost is not just Peter's sermon, but everyone witnessing;

† Jails were opened, by groups praying;

† Miracles happened as the group met and prayed;

† In Christian Relationships, miracles still happen;

The story of the <u>Velveteen Rabbit</u> is of a new stuffed rabbit in the play room who talks to an old loved stuffed horse. The wise old stuffed horse talked to the new rabbit toy about the place. He told of many new mechanical toys that had come, get broken, and be thrown away. But the older toys became "real" to children. "It isn't how you are made, it's what happens to you when a child loves you over a long time, not just to play with, but to live with"; The old horse with patches, joints stitched, loss of hair and eyes dropping out, was loved by the children. "That makes you real – It's something you become".

† ***Steps in the Water*** – do action, exercise your faith, - <u>Do Faith Work</u>

I receive a magazine called "Faith Works," that seeks to tell of Christians who put their faith and commitments to work in real-time life.

† Those Israelites could find many reasons not to act on their faith and commitment.

† The water was high, at flood stage, the wrong time,

† The water was dirty, muddy;

† They were dressed up, let's go back and change; But God told them that the test of their faith was to "step in the water".

† The miracle happened only after they stepped in the water – the waters parted!

† The real miracle for them was the exercising of faith, stepping in the water.

† Following Jesus is not just knowing the right things, or talking the right way, it is in doing our faith.

† Book of James challenges us – show me your faith by your works. We have made following Jesus a set of words, phrases, titles, and creeds, - a world of words.

† Real "life" faith is lived in doing faith.

In the Olympics in Atlanta, we watched a special moment when 4'9", 87 pound Kerri Strung was carried by her coach to receive a gold medal. The U.S. had a thin lead, and only Kerri remained to win or lose it; her vault was that important. On her first try she fell, twisting an ankle and tearing two ligaments. Composing herself, whispering a prayer and repeating the words, "I will, I will", she charged down the runway. She vaulted, twisting in the air, and landed on her injured ankle. But she held herself upright for the second needed for this to count. She received one of the highest scores in the meet, and won the gold medal for her team and her nation.

How are you "doing" your faith? When it's rough?

When you are hurt? When others don't agree?

"Faith is the substance of things hoped for, the evidence of things now seen."

We are substance, evidence of Jesus, How are we doing?